Making more Changes

Editor's Choice

Edited by Mary Lou Santovec

Magna Publications, Inc.
Madison, WI 53704

Magna Publications, Inc.
2718 Dryden Drive
Madison, WI 53704-3086
800/433-0499

Cover design by Tamara L. Cook and Erin Stark

Library of Congress Cataloging-in-Publication

Making more changes: editor's choice/ edited by Mary Lou Santovec.

    p. cm.

Includes bibliographical references and index.

ISBN 0-912150-37-8 (pbk.)

    1. College students--Recruiting--United States--Case studies.
2. Minority college students--Recruiting--United States--Case
studies. 3. College dropouts--United States--Case studies.
I. Santovec, Mary Lou, 1954- . II. Recruitment and retention.
LB2342.82.M36 1996
378.1'05--dc20   95-9383

                                        CIP

Table of Contents

Table of Contents
continued

Introduction

Introduction

Welcome to *Making More Changes: Editor's Choice*. This book is a compilation of articles from the past five years of our *Recruitment and Retention* newsletter. We chose these articles to represent the types of topics covered in *Recruitment and Retention*, as well as for their relevance today.

To ensure that the information in each article in this compilation is up-to-date, we sent copies of the original article to the individual(s) cited, asking for new information, corrections, or updates. Our thanks go to these people who helped improve this book.

Using the Book

For your convenience — and to make this book more user-friendly — we've added a matrix to help you find the articles most appropriate for your situation. For example, if you're interested in reading about programs that target both adults and minorities, refer to the matrix for those shaded in both boxes. Likewise, if you're simply interested in athletes, refer to the programs checked under that category.

All articles printed prior to 1994 were updated. Some changes were minor and merely incorporated in the text. When massive changes occurred, a separate "Update" section was included. At the very end of each article we added the date when the article was first published.

Current Trends in Recruitment and Retention

Since the first of these stories appeared in 1990, many changes have taken place in higher education, especially in recruitment. Student expectations, declining institutional budgets, rising tuition, and intense public scrutiny are affecting the way colleges and universities do business.

While recruiting and retaining students for a multicultural and diverse campus are still important goals, higher education is having to answer questions about their cost in terms of fairness from those who feel threatened by affirmative action policies. Despite the heroic efforts of many faculty, staff, and administrators, this attitude causes a chilly climate for minority students on many campuses and a push for separatism rather than inclusion.

This more vocal attitude can be traced, at least indirectly, to the cost of higher education and the importance of a college degree to future employability. The elimination of many blue-collar jobs and demand for post-high school education for most entry-level positions mean that more students from diverse backgrounds than ever before are attending colleges and universities.

Couple that with ever-rising tuition rates and no guarantee that a college degree is the ticket to well-paid employment — especially positions with salaries high enough to pay off the debt that many students are facing when they graduate — and you have part of the recipe for the current climate of intolerance.

The changing expectations of students are also impacting the way colleges recruit and retain them. In the March/April 1994 issue of *Change: The Magazine of Higher Learning*, David C. Smith, director of admissions at Syracuse U., summed up the prevailing attitude this way: "Colleges have entered the same level of marketplace now as durable goods, with the consumer asking, 'Am I getting what I'm paying for?' We used to hear about education as a good investment; now we hear about higher education as just one more necessary expenditure; so people shop — and aggressively — for price comparisons among colleges of similar perceived quality."

As a result of this, there seems to be a trend for disappointed students — those who've been denied admission to a particular college or who've received a low grade in one of their classes — to choose litigation to ease their pain of rejection. The number of instances is rising and getting much more media attention.

Also impacting student recruitment and retention are the students themselves, specifically those from single-parent homes, and those with emotional problems, as well as alcohol and substance abuse in their backgrounds. These students are leading colleges and universities to rethink their policies for students with previous felony convictions, as well as con-firmed cases of alcohol and drug abuse. Some institutions have added a question on their admissions applications about previous convictions. Others are putting in place new pro-grams to serve the needs of students with criminal records or substance abuse in their backgrounds.

The face of the student body is changing, with older students and part-time students becoming the new majority. Approximately 85% of the non-traditional students attend college part-time. Estimates are that it will take most of these students eight years to obtain a bachelor's degree.

Another hot topic during the past five years — and one that seems to be getting hotter — is the pressure on admissions officers to fill a class. Judging from the frequency with which admissions directors are changing jobs, it almost seems as if they have less job security than NCAA Division I coaches. The reality of this insecurity often translates into occasional bouts of questionable ethics because of the constant pressure to produce or else.

External forces, particularly changes in funding, have forced institutions to confront the issue of accountability, leading many schools to apply business philosophies such as Total Quality Management (TQM) and re-engineering to higher education. TQM, a business philosophy made famous by the teachings of W. Edwards Deming, looks at continuously improving a particular process and emphasizes identifying and fulfilling the customers' needs. re-engineering looks at the core processes and radically redesigns them in order to dramatically improve an organization's competitiveness.

The adoption of these philosophies means it's no longer acceptable to say, "That's the way we've always done it." But looking at students as customers requires a paradigm shift in the way institutions do business.

Future Trends

Accountability isn't only hitting higher education. There's a tremendous push for reform at the K-12 level as well. Such things as charter schools, school choice, and outcomes-based education will directly impact how colleges and universities make admissions decisions in the future.

Controversy surrounding the potential gender and ethnic bias of standardized tests has more colleges and universities now making them an optional part of a student's portfolio for admission. A decrease in reliance on grades as well as test scores will influence the way future admissions decisions are made.

The Internet is rapidly changing the way colleges and universities fulfill their mission. At this writing, more than 600 postsecondary institutions have set up shop in the form of a "home page" on the World Wide Web, with more pages being created daily.

Some institutions are using the Internet for distance education — everything from one course to an entire degree. For example, the University of Phoenix (AZ) and Louisiana College (LA) have begun offering undergraduate degrees via the Net. And the University of Memphis (TN) and New York University will offer full graduate degrees through an interactive network. Colleges and universities will have to develop different ways of serving the needs of these "virtual" students.

Whatever the future holds, the only thing we can be sure of is that it will be different from today. *Making More Changes* offers an overview of where we've been over the past five years. And we at *Recruitment and Retention* will bring you the future as it unfolds.

Mary Lou Santovec
Editor

Matrix

How to Use the Matrix

Across the top of the matrix are several categories. Choose a category of interest to you, follow the column down until you reach a shaded area. Then follow the horizontal row to the left to find an article related to that category. Follow the column further to find other articles.

	Advising	Adult Students	Athletes	Budget Innovation	Disabilities	Distance Learning	Diversity	Ethnic Minorities	Evaluation	Freshmen	Juniors	Marketing	Mentoring	Orientation	Parents/Family	Research	Residence Halls	Sophomores	Summer Programs	Technology	TQM	Transfers	Volunteers	Women
Great Ideas Contest Winners	▓			▓			▓	▓				▓		▓		▓	▓	▓	▓	▓	▓	▓	▓	▓
A Model for Creating Diversity							▓	▓			▓		▓	▓										
Success CAAPs Off a Summer Bridge Program	▓	▓						▓						▓					▓					
Playing Games Leads to Academic Success	▓																			▓				
Recruitment Strategies	▓	▓	▓		▓							▓		▓		▓	▓	▓				▓		▓
Adult Students: Where to Find Them and How to Serve Them		▓										▓												
Institutions Serve Non-Traditional Learners	▓	▓										▓		▓										▓

	Advising	Adult Students	Athletes	Budget Innovation	Disabilities	Distance Learning	Diversity	Ethnic Minorities	Evaluation	Freshmen	Juniors	Marketing	Mentoring	Orientation	Parents/Family	Research	Residence Halls	Sophomores	Summer Programs	Technology	TQM	Transfers	Volunteers	Women
"Relationship Management" Impacts Enrollment	■											■												
Schools Cut Recruitment Costs				■								■												
Chicago State University: Recruitment & Retention Begin at the Top	■												■											
Students Take Five and Broaden Their Horizons	■			■																				
Improving Productivity through Performance Management																								
San Juan College Thinks "Culture" When Recruiting Native Americans							■	■				■			■									
Ohio State University Works to Attract Minority Graduate Students								■											■					
Faculty/Admissions Office Partnership Changes Recruiting Focus													■											

	Advising	Adult Students	Athletes	Budget Innovation	Disabilities	Distance Learning	Diversity	Ethnic Minorities	Evaluation	Freshmen	Juniors	Marketing	Mentoring	Orientation	Parents/Family	Research	Residence Halls	Sophomores	Summer Programs	Technology	TQM	Transfers	Volunteers	Women
Employees Get on the Line for Triton College				▨								▨											▨	
The Proof Is in the Advertising				▨								▨												
Original Marketing Helps Saint Vincent College Meet Its Goals				▨								▨												
Key Steps in Working Successfully with Alumni Volunteers																							▨	
Collaboration Makes Transfers "Supergraduates"								▨							▨				▨			▨		
College Quality: More Than a Ranking	▨								▨	▨														
Address Correction Requested: Personalizing Direct Mail												▨												
Ethical Technology Increases Delivery Options																				▨				
Recruitment with a "Flip of the Switch"																				▨				

	Advising	Adult Students	Athletes	Budget Innovation	Disabilities	Distance Learning	Diversity	Ethnic Minorities	Evaluation	Freshmen	Juniors	Marketing	Mentoring	Orientation	Parents/Family	Research	Residence Halls	Sophomores	Summer Programs	Technology	TQM	Transfers	Volunteers	Women
Video Brings Four-Year Campuses to Future Transfer Students																				▓		▓		
Database Provides Access to Distance Learning Opportunities						▓																		
PRIZM Helps Refine Search												▓								▓				
College Encourages "Test Drive" of Academic Computer																				▓				
Effective Telemarketing Boosts Commuter College's Growth												▓								▓				
Creative Computer Technology Invades Admissions Office				▓																▓		▓		
TQM Changes Admissions from Impossible to Accomplished																					▓			
Contract Provides Second Chance																						▓		

Retention Strategies

Retention Strategies	Advising	Adult Students	Athletes	Budget Innovation	Disabilities	Distance Learning	Diversity	Ethnic Minorities	Evaluation	Freshmen	Juniors	Marketing	Mentoring	Orientation	Parents/Family	Research	Residence Halls	Sophomores	Summer Programs	Technology	TQM	Transfers	Volunteers	Women
Retain Adults by Addressing their Feelings of Impostorship		▉																						
Orientation Program Is "For Adults Only"		▉																						
Community College Builds "Bridge" for Minority Adults		▉						▉																
Advisors Beat the Budget Cut Blues	▉			▨										▉										
Alpha Gives Undecided Students a Sense of Identity	▉												▉	▉										
Necessity Is the Mother of Invention	▉			▨										▉										
Developmental Advising "Hallmark of Retention"	▉									▉													▉	
Mini-Advising Center Supports Undecided Majors	▉																							

	Advising	Adult Students	Athletes	Budget Innovation	Disabilities	Distance Learning	Diversity	Ethnic Minorities	Evaluation	Freshmen	Juniors	Marketing	Mentoring	Orientation	Parents/Family	Research	Residence Halls	Sophomores	Summer Programs	Technology	TQM	Transfers	Volunteers	Women
Theories of Relativity: Enlisting Family Members as Co-Advisors	■													■										
Program Builds Academic Success for Student Athletes	■		■																					
What to Do When There Are Too Many Students, Too Few Counselors	■			■																				
Neglected Minorities					■		■												■					
Overlooked Minorities: Disabled Students	■				■		■	■																
Suggestions for Managing Cultural Diversity in the Classroom							■	■																
Center Restores Academic Hope	■												■											
Don't Forget the Parents														■										

	Advising	Adult Students	Athletes	Budget Innovation	Disabilities	Distance Learning	Diversity	Ethnic Minorities	Evaluation	Freshmen	Juniors	Marketing	Mentoring	Orientation	Parents/Family	Research	Residence Halls	Sophomores	Summer Programs	Technology	TQM	Transfers	Volunteers	Women
Dead Lecture Society Enlivens Faculty-Student Relationships													X				X							
Finding the Answers	X			X										X					X					
Retention: A Campuswide Responsibility	X																							
Mentoring Program Helps Disadvantaged Nursing Students	X												X											
Service, Satisfaction, and Advocacy: Xavier's Freshman Retention Program	X									X			X	X										
The Rise and Fall of a Model First-Year Program	X									X				X										
Game Simulates Freshman Year										X														
Academic STARS							X	X					X											
High-Tech Future for Minorities								X												X				

Article	Women	Volunteers	Transfers	TQM	Technology	Summer Programs	Sophomores	Residence Halls	Research	Parents/Family	Orientation	Mentoring	Marketing	Juniors	Freshmen	Evaluation	Ethnic Minorities	Diversity	Distance Learning	Disabilities	Budget Innovation	Athletes	Adult Students	Advising
Research Yields Retention Data										■														
Attachment vs. Independence: The High School to College Transition	■									■					■									
Beating the Sophomore Slump						■	■																	■
Give Students "True" Responsibility and They'll Manage Themselves								■																
Residence Hall Improves Grades								■																
Residence Facilities and Retention	■							■																
Survey Measures Transition Stress									■						■									
Volunteers Strive to "Advise Five"		■																			■			■
Scholarship Requires a Commitment to Diversity																		■						

	Advising	Adult Students	Athletes	Budget Innovation	Disabilities	Distance Learning	Diversity	Ethnic Minorities	Evaluation	Freshmen	Juniors	Marketing	Mentoring	Orientation	Parents/Family	Research	Residence Halls	Sophomores	Summer Programs	Technology	TQM	Transfers	Volunteers	Women
An "Electronic Forum" Gives Voice to the Silent																				■				
Computerized System Improves Advising, Saves Money	■																			■				
College Makes Students "Job 1"																					■			

Great Ideas
Contest Winners

Section One

A Model for Creating Diversity

While recruiting minority students for an undergraduate degree is often a challenge, the laws of supply and demand make recruiting them for graduate school even tougher, particularly for campuses with low minority enrollment. But the Graduate Scholars program at Indiana University of Pennsylvania offers a good model for creating diversity at a predominantly white, rural campus.

Begun in 1983 with just two students, the program has since grown to support 90 full-time minority master's and doctoral candidates — about 10% of IUP's student body.

The heart of the program is a guaranteed, full-tuition waiver and a stipend (ranging from $4,410 to $6,000) that supports the students for as long as they're enrolled at IUP. The waiver also covers up to five undergraduate credits if the students need the courses.

Valarie Mancuso, assistant dean, admits that's quite a difference from IUP's other assistantship contracts, which are one year in length and cover only graduate school credits. "The campus has been very supportive of the need for a diverse climate," she explains.

However, no amount of financial support will help retain students who feel unwelcome. So Mancuso and two graduate assistants work to ensure that IUP meets all the needs of these students.

Before arriving on campus, future students receive letters from the graduate assistants inviting them to an informal orientation, which introduces them to the campus and to each other. At orientation, representatives from administration, career services, and housing share relevant information.

Later that day, Mancuso's office hosts a wine and cheese reception; the guest list includes minority faculty and administrators, and current minority graduate students to help build bridges and offer support. "The older students are always pretty eager to take the younger ones under their wings," says Mancuso.

All students are invited twice each semester to luncheons designated as social and networking experiences, but which also act as early warning signals, helping Mancuso and her staff to identify and ward off potential problems. During the semester, the graduate assistants keep in touch with the students with lots of letters and organize informal students-only social activities, such as potluck dinners and bowling parties. Students fund the students-only activities; the Graduate School provides prizes to winners of the events.

Recruitment Strategies

To attract potential students, Mancuso uses the GRE Minority Locator Service, attends conferences, and hosts visiting undergraduates interested in the university. She also works closely with the McNair Program at Bowie State University (MD), a predominantly black institution.

An annual marketing and recruitment competition supports academic departments in their efforts to recruit students. Each department submits a plan — which may incorporate brochures, campus visits, or advertising in national publications — to the graduate school, which reviews the plans for funding. Each plan must include a component specifically targeted toward recruiting minorities.

Despite changes in presidential leadership over the years, the Graduate Scholars program has always been supported. And so far, the university hasn't put a cap on the number of Graduate Scholars it can support. Mancuso attributes this support to the program's 81% retention rate and the more than 250 minority students who've graduated from IUP in the past 11 years. "It's proven itself," she says.

For more information, contact:

Valarie Mancuso, Assistant Dean, The Graduate School and Research, Indiana University of Pennsylvania, Stright Hall, Indiana, PA 15705-1081; Ph: 412/357-2222. (October 1994)

Success CAAPs Off a Summer Bridge Program

The summer between the freshman and sophomore years is a tenuous one, particularly for students whose first year was less than successful academically. But a program at Marygrove College (MI) increases the likelihood that students will give college another try.

As an urban, commuter institution with the highest percentage of African American students of any four-year liberal arts college in the country (excluding the historically black colleges), Marygrove serves a population that's substantially part-time, first-generation, and older — a population often at-risk and attrition-prone.

Kathleen Tkach, assistant dean of students, reports: "A typical Marygrove student is an African American woman in her early 30's, who's employed and commutes to the college daily. She may also be the first member of her family to attend college."

To help improve retention and assist these students in completing their education, Marygrove has instituted a number of programs:

- Basic skills placement testing
- Foundational and developmental studies programs for those whose academic skills need work
- A "First Semester Program" — extended orientation
- A learning skills center
- Intrusive academic advising
- Peer mentoring
- Extensive financial aid and counseling programs
- Active monitoring of student progress and student service programs
- A system to stay in touch with students during the summer break
- Regular opportunities for students to meet with role models

Despite these initiatives, Marygrove found that there were students who, at the end of their first year, needed additional assistance. So in 1992, the college applied for and received a grant from the Minority Equity Program of the Michigan Department of Education to fund the Summer Career and Academic Assistance Program (CAAP).

CAAP is a voluntary, tuition-free, non-credit, supplementary summer bridge program for students who've completed their first year, but are on probation or have been encouraged by one or more of their instructors, to develop their academic skills.

During the first year, CAAP students came to campus five days per week for eight weeks. In the mornings, they worked at on-campus jobs, for example, in the admissions office calling prospective students. Their afternoons were spent in the classroom — in small-group, tutorial sessions that covered math, writing, and reading. One afternoon a week was devoted to exploring careers and setting goals. Students were paid $5/hour for their work performance and class attendance.

In 1993, Marygrove eliminated the work, career exploration, and payment portions of the program and shortened its delivery time to two mornings per week for six weeks, which significantly changed the face of the program and forced them to evaluate whether or not those components were important to the success of the program. Tkach explains why: "The first summer, the promise of work [and payment] was used as a hook to encourage students to come. From the program evaluation, we found that the students were just as willing to come without the work portion and more willing to come because the program was less than a full day." She adds: "Although the work portion was valuable, we felt our money was better spent broadening the base of the CAAP program."

Originally, students took one hour each of math, reading, and writing. "Now," says Tkach, "there's a more modular schedule. Students have to enroll for at least two hours and they get to choose what they want to work on. They can take two hours of math if they want."

The program is administered entirely in-house by staff in several offices, including advising, career services, learning skills center, and student affairs. Marygrove faculty, who are paid a stipend, teach the basic skills courses.

Eliminating the work component has made program administration easier, admits Tkach. "Now if a student doesn't come to campus, they don't improve their skills. When we had the work component, we had to deal with time sheets and making sure students showed up for their jobs."

Of those eligible for CAAP, approximately 50% took advantage of it — 95% of whom were African Americans. Statistics reveal that 79% of the 1992 CAAP students returned for their sophomore year, while 88% of the 1993 participants returned, compared with total student body rates of 58% and 57%. For the 1992 CAAP students, 59% returned for their junior year.

Program costs range from $6,000-7,000 or about $100 per student. Since the program "saves" 10-15 students per year, Tkach notes, "we couldn't afford not to do it."

For more information, contact:

Kathleen Tkach, Assistant Dean of Students, Marygrove College, 8425 W. McNichols Rd., Detroit, MI 48221; Ph: 313/862-8000, ext. 388. (September 1994)

Playing Games Leads to Academic Success

For new students, the lure of newfound friends, parties, and freedoms frequently eclipses their academic responsibilities. If students regularly yield to those temptations, they soon discover the negative impact on their grades and eventually their academic success.

How do you make students understand the implications of their behavior *before* they flunk out? A computer simulation game developed by Texas Tech's James Gregory and implemented by John Rivera illustrates the consequences of students' actions.

The Grade Results Evaluation Game (GREG) is a learning model that's based on analyzing a student's most difficult course. "If students can develop a strategy to help them succeed in that course," says Rivera, "they can apply that strategy to less difficult courses."

The game uses mathematical models to help students numerically simulate the effects of time and study management choices on academic performance. Its objective: to teach them how to be successful and show them how to obtain the highest grades with the least amount of study time.

GREG also allows students to test alternative learning ideas without the risk of failing a class. "We empower the students to help themselves," says Rivera. "We want them to discover how to learn and what things they can do themselves to help them learn."

Teaching Students How to Learn

The DOS-based, menu-driven software examines the structure of learning and the principles that govern the learning process. In developing the software, Gregory's intent was to have students interact with it, not just sit passively and watch. Research shows that this is more effective than having an advisor "advise them" how to study and/or "tell" them what to do.

To determine their probability for success in a class, students enter data using five menus — financial analysis, time analysis, study management, student management analysis, and course structure. They're asked to reveal such things as their finances (including whether they have to work to pay for their education), the time they use for sleeping, dating, recreation, whether they study with a group or individually, and the efficiency of their teachers.

"While students can't control the efficiency of their teachers," admits Rivera, "it does impact performance. A good teacher is engaging and students feel free to ask questions."

Each screen has a built-in default value. For example, on the class attendance screen in the study management menu, Rivera and Gregory assume the student will attend class 100% of the time, so that screen defaults at 100%.

Students are asked to enter data based on their own experiences. They can choose to keep the original numerical values or change them to more closely resemble their reality. "We're not telling them what to do," Rivera explains. "We want them to just put down what they actually do."

"Sometimes, [on the attendance screen] when the student doesn't put down 100, we find out that maybe there are other factors at work, like the student has given up on the class because they're hopelessly behind or they attempted something they're not ready for yet."

After the data is entered, the software simulates results for students' current academic situations. As they try alternative strategies by varying what they enter, students discover that "perhaps 24 hours a week of watching television is too much," Rivera observes.

The results show how much time students have available for their education — helping prevent them from overloads. "We all have the same amount of time," explains Rivera. "How they use this time directly impacts how well they do."

The software predicts three results:

- The estimated test score for the current course that's being evaluated
- The estimated time it will take for the student to earn that test score
- The estimated GPA

The software calculates to one-half of a point the grades students have received in the past, showing the students the validity of the tool.

For at-risk students, Rivera and Gregory have discovered that coupling the software with counseling and follow-up sessions to check on students' academic progress improved.

Rivera credits the software for the ability to counsel students without the stigma often attached to counseling. Because students have to be taught how to use the software, "it's a good way for me to talk to them without students realizing they're revealing stuff that they may not want to reveal," says Rivera. "You get information by listening that you wouldn't ordinarily get — outside factors that impact on their success."

Rivera's method to encourage the students to followup may seem a little unusual, but it works. "They don't get to print out their results on John's [Rivera] computer," Gregory explains. "He explains to them that he has labels set up in his printer and that he can't take them out because he's in the middle of printing a list." The students then have to go to the campus learning center and reuse the program on their own and bring back a printout.

The lack of egos involved in GREG/Counseling is evident when Rivera eagerly credits Gregory for the software's success. "He developed GREG on his own time, out of his own experiences with minority students, and without any grant funding," explains Rivera.

Gregory's inspiration occurred after hearing noted Berkeley mathematician Philip Uri Treisman speak about his research on the success of students who worked in groups. Curiosity about what other factors influenced student success and learning led Gregory to test his hypothesis and develop the game.

Rivera willingly took the tool and used it with students, pointing out that Gregory gave him the freedom to determine how best to use it. Together, Rivera, Gregory, and other colleagues exchange information on the results and discuss improvements to the product.

One principle that Gregory incorporated into the software relates to timing. Research on study patterns shows that students who study material learned in class immediately after class will retain more of the material than if they were to wait until later to study their notes.

That principle is part of the mantra Rivera impresses on students as one of the keys to success. He encourages the students to "study immediately, study repeatedly, study collaboratively," remarking that "it's just dramatic how much the retention of material drops off the later they review it."

Initially developed in 1991 to help students in the Minority Engineering Program, GREG/Counseling has been used during summer training sessions with minority students for the past three years. In 1994, the college of engineering received a small grant to expand the use of GREG/Counseling to other minority students.

Because the software was calibrated against data collected from K-12 schools as well as college students, future plans include using it with students in area high schools. It's a requirement for students on probation to use the software and attend the follow-up sessions before they're allowed to register.

The Results

In Spring 1993, 62% of the students who used the software and counseling system achieved a GPA of 2.0 or better, compared with only 18% without it. Students who used it during Fall 1993 achieved similar results. Those who used GREG and had three or more follow-up counseling sessions all had GPAs of 2.0 or better. The average GPA prior to this was 1.67.

Rivera and Gregory estimate that approximately 30 students have been saved from academic failure using GREG/Counseling. "Our goal is to serve the West Texas area, which is made up of 60% minorities and rural white students," explains Rivera. "If we're going to succeed with these students, we have to take them where they're at and work with them."

For more information, contact:

John Rivera, Director of Student Relations, College of Engineering, Box 43103, or James Gregory, Department of Civil Engineering, Box 41023, Texas Tech U., Lubbock, TX 79409; Ph: 806/742-3451 (Rivera) or 742-3488 (Gregory). (August 1994)

To order a copy of the GREG software, instructions, and papers on the essential elements of learning and teacher efficiency, contact:

James Gregory at the above address to order the software. Kendall-Hunt Publishers (IA) plans to publish a user manual that will be distributed with the software.

Recruitment
Strategies

Section Two

Adult Students: Where to Find Them and How to Serve Them

Baby boomers, because of their numbers, are one of the largest attractive target for college recruiters. How do you reach these prospective students? Joan Schwartz, Program Director at the American Council on Education's Center for Adult Learning and Educational Credentials, has identified "populations that are eager to return to school with a little prompting and support."

Where to Find Them

Adult learners are to be found everywhere — in the military, in business and industry, government and volunteer agencies, and as members of national associations. Currently, approximately only 23% of the American population over the age of 25 holds a four-year baccalaureate degree. That means that 78% of the adult population are potential students. Of course not all the population is interested in earning a degree, but they might be interested in attending courses to upgrade their employment skills, to further their career paths and/or to enrich their lives.

The military represents a major source of potential students: a population of some two million, with 750,000 in the Army alone. Nearly one-third of service members rotate out of the military each year. After discharge, 87% return home. "That means every college and university will have returning veterans," says Schwartz. And most of them come with funding.

Over 90% of veterans are enrolled in educational benefits programs that provide them with $12,000 to $24,000 in tuition money. There are other reasons why veterans are an attractive group to recruit. Minorities and women are well-represented and during their term of enlistment the military tries to imbue them with the need and desire for further education. Schwartz feels that "they're constantly encouraged to take college classes and ultimately earn a college degree and they come with a certain set of desirable characteristics that you'll find younger students don't necessarily have."

With the advent of the Army/ACE Registry Transcript System (AARTS), schools now find it much easier to award credit to Army soldiers and veterans. The AARTS transcript simplifies acceptance of college credit recommendations for learning acquired in the military. "The transcript, a computerized record of all the soldier's education and training, including the ACE credit recommendations, gives the soldier or veteran a document that can be handed to a college official for immediate evaluation," said Schwartz.

Another source of potential students that recruiters can tap into are businesses, industry, government and volunteer organizations. These organizations are an attractive group to approach because they oftentimes offer tuition reimbursement to their employees, space for on-location classes, and encouragement and support to those employees wanting to take college courses and/or degrees. Recruiters can obtain the names of organizations already interested in promoting employee college attendance by reviewing the *National Guide to Educational Credit for Training Programs*, the courses directory for the ACE Program on Non-Collegiate Sponsored Instruction (PONSI).

PONSI evaluates the organization's courses, using a process similar to the one used in the military evaluations program. Over the last 20 years, hundreds of organizations have had their courses evaluated for possible college-level credit. Interested organizations can contact ACE for information about how they can arrange to have their courses evaluated for college-level credit recommendations. The organizations provide ACE with annual course updates and receive a course re-evaluation every five years.

Recruiters can also approach national organizations that offer certification examinations. Some of these organizations have had their examinations evaluated by ACE for college level credit recommendations. This evaluation offers their membership an attractive benefit for career and educational advancement.

Schools recruiting individuals who have completed ACE-evaluated courses or examinations find that these students are highly motivated, know that they are able to do the coursework, and are eager learners, explained Schwartz.

The ACE-sponsored evaluation programs also benefit the participating organizations by helping them stretch their tuition reimbursement dollars. The acceptance of the ACE credit recommendations offers to save tuition dollars, it offers a benefit to individuals in all the various organizations, and the organization becomes a supporter of lifelong learning.

How to Serve Them

Schwartz offers some advice for schools interested in recruiting adults: "It's imperative that the president and/or dean are committed to supporting adult learning programs offered at their institutions. Their commitment and support send a message that adult learners are an important population. This positively articulated support will influence faculty perceptions."

A formal, written policy concerning the acceptance of nontraditional learning is crucial. Adult's main concerns are time and money. If there is no recognition of the learning that has taken place outside the college classroom, adults will be much less willing to attend your institution.

Make the student feel welcome. Have services offered in the evening, i.e., open house visits and office hours for administrative and counseling services. Also, have faculty participate in the school's outreach activities. Try to have those faculty who like working with adults participate in open house evenings and orientation days for new students.

Provide proper conditions for making learning occur. Research about how adults learn indicates that comfortable physical surroundings, relevance of learning, and an individual's participation in the learning experience are necessary for learning to occur. Schwartz also recommends that schools develop resource centers and introductory classes to help adults overcome their fear of college. "After all, if they had no fears of attending college, they would have been there years ago."

For more information, contact:

Joan Schwartz, Program Director, Center for Adult Learning and Educational Credentials, American Council on Education, 1 Dupont Circle, Suite 250, Washington, DC 20036; Ph: 202/939-9432. (May 91)

For further reading:

Aurand, Tim, "Segmenting the Adult Learning Market," *Adult Learning,* January/February 1984, pp. 16-18.

College Board, *100 Ways to Serve Adults,* 1990, New York, NY.

Greenberg, Elinor Miller, "It's Really Quite Simple: Meeting the Needs of Diverse Adult Learners," *Liberal Education*, Vol. 78, No. 4, September/October 1992, pp. 2-7.

Sanders, Neill, and Parfetto, Gret, "Information Needs of Adult Learners," *The Journal of College Admission*, Winter 1993, pp. 11-17.

Schlossberg, et al, *Improving Higher Education Environments for Adults*, Jossey-Bass, 1989, San Francisco.

Snyder, Brenda, "Adult Students: Who Are We and What do We Need?" *Liberal Education*, Vol. 78, No. 4, September/October 1992, pp. 46-48.

Institutions Serve Non-Traditional Learners

Thanks to the Baby Boom, the number of students age 25 and older in postsecondary institutions rose 59% between 1974 and 1988. An analysis of the College Board's 1980 study of adult learners noted that *change* was their primary motivator: adults begin or continue their education in order to cope with transitions in their lives. By understanding the motivations of adult learners, schools can develop special programs that help them succeed.

College Moves Women toward a Four-Year Degree

Everett Community College's (WA) year-long, learning community effort encourages women to set their educational goals high. "Women on the Move to a Four-Year Degree Learning Community" is a writing-intensive, integrated studies program that offers a structured series of classes — exclusively for program participants — in addition to a twice-weekly seminar with instructors from each of their classes. The Women on the Move enter a preplanned program consisting of pre-college English remediation, transferable college courses, college success strategies, and support services. Laura Hedges, Director of the Women's Center, says, "The Women on the Move Learning Community provides faculty and peer support so that students can overcome fears of returning to school after 5, 10, 15 — even 20 to 30 years of being absent from the educational environment and to gain a sense of themselves and their abilities."

Women on the Move (WOM) helps those who know they want a four-year degree as well as those who are unsure. Its format provides students with the necessary skills to track their own programs. Hedges explains, "Even after the program ends, the students continue to take classes together.

They have formed lifelong friendships and heightened their self-esteem and formulated goals."

During the first quarter of WOM, faculty pair English and sociology or psychology classes, enabling students to write across the curriculum and work on dual assignments and tests. An Orientation to College seminar covers topics that include study skills, learning styles, critical thinking, self-esteem, and other college success strategies. "The first quarter looks at students and their lives," says Hedges. "The goal is to be able to relate their learning to their life experiences as well as to look at the experiences of other students."

Interpersonal communications or psychology, English 101, math, and the seminar make up the second quarter. The third quarter consists of environmental sciences, English 102, math, and the seminar. Faculty evaluate the students' math skills so they can work at an appropriate level. The program strongly emphasizes math and science careers.

Faculty commitment and support is key. Instructors who volunteer for the program meet weekly to brainstorm intervention strategies and monitor each student's progress. "The faculty accept a smaller class load in exchange for the additional time and energy spent in the learning community. But," Hedges adds, "the program has its inherent rewards in working with students who learn, grow, and blossom."

A $2,000 seed grant from the Washington Center for Improving the Quality of Undergraduate Education enabled Women on the Move to get off the ground in 1987. The grant has since returned to the program to subsidize transportation for students to visit four-year campuses and for faculty to attend workshops on developing learning communities.

Now in its seventh year, the Women on the Move Learning Community five-year study indicated that Women on the Move represent, non-traditional students who face greater disadvantage and challenges, but do better in every aspect than non-Women on the Move students. They achieve higher GPAs, graduate more quickly, and continue their lives with greater skills and experiences.

Mentors Help Individualize Learning

Most educators know that learning can occur at any time, in any place. But few are willing to base up to 75% of a bachelor's degree on that premise. At Empire State College

— one of the SUNY system's most unusual institutions — faculty mentors help students "sort out what life has added up to at this point," says Timothy Lehmann, Director of the National Center on Adult Learning at Empire State College, "and see what type of learning can be extracted from past experience."

Empire State was created in 1971 to "serve those who couldn't be served effectively on a regular campus." Its strength lies in its ability to custom-tailor education to fit the needs of adult students — through credit for prior learning, independent study, learning contracts, and on-site faculty mentors. "The pace and amount of learning varies, depending upon work and lifestyle," explains Lehmann.

One of the college's unique features is that it's a public institution with a statewide mission. Over 40 regional centers and units cover New York state, allowing Empire to tap into the resources — faculty as well as facilities — of the other SUNY campuses. "When the campus was designed, the goal was to draw upon the resources of the state system, but not duplicate them," says Lehmann. "With Empire, the whole idea of a fixed campus has been turned around to allow the campus to offer outreach to the students."

The heart of the individualized education is a one-to-one relationship between faculty mentor and student. When students enroll, Empire assigns mentors who help them plan and coordinate a course of study. Besides teaching, mentors also act as advisors, help students develop learning contracts, identify instructional resources, and evaluate their progress.

To earn a degree, students must successfully complete a series of learning contracts, each of which includes goals, activities, a description of how the contract fits into the student's overall program, and evaluation methods. A learning contract may involve an audio-visual course designed for self-study, travel experiences with a specific study plan, an internship, or even new responsibilities at work.

The program includes checks for quality. After the student creates — with the help of a mentor — a degree plan, it's reviewed for content and quality by an on-site faculty committee.

A broad, multidisciplinary curriculum encompassing 11 areas of study meets the diverse needs of Empire's 7000 students. The typical Empire student is 37 years old, independent, self-directed, and part-time. "Between 60% and 75% of new students come from referrals from former students and graduates," says Lehmann. "Because of 'grapevine knowledge,' there's a self-selection process, so most are pretty committed by the time they enroll."

Studies of Empire graduates show the individualized approach works. Between 55% and 60% go on to graduate studies, which, Lehmann adds, "is unusual, considering most of the students are at least 40 years old when they finish their undergraduate work."

For more information, contact:

Laura Hedges, Director of the Women's Center, Everett Community College, 801 Wetmore, Everett, WA 98201; Ph: 206/388-9293 or Timothy Lehmann, Associate Vice President for Research and Evaluation, Empire State College, 28 Union Ave., Saratoga Springs, NY 12866; Ph: 518/587-2100 ext. 287. (December 1990)

"Relationship Management" Impacts Enrollment

In 1992, when Franklin University (OH) asked, "What can we do to improve our service to students?" they got their answer from an unusual source — a local bank.

Franklin met with representatives from the Huntington Bank, who introduced the concept of "relationship management" — the setting and meeting of expectations between service-provider and client — which the bank uses in its successful personal banking program.

"After the meeting, we asked ourselves, 'Why can't we have a personal banker for every student?' — someone they can connect with regarding financial aid, course selection, and registration?" says Linda Steele, Vice President for Students.

Originally, incoming students would work with an admissions counselor through registration. Afterwards, they'd be assigned an advisor who would take care of them for the next four years.

"We wanted to streamline the change going from one area to another. We wanted to establish a relationship so the student doesn't have to start over again [after registration]," Steele says.

Franklin's solution: merge admissions with advising and separate out the recruiting component.

The former admissions counselors and advisors became a team of 10 Student Services Associates (SSAs) — seven of whom are full-time — who address the needs of Franklin's 4,000 students.

With the restructuring, the university was able to easily ascertain what skills each group needed and so hire different types of people for each job — sales-oriented marketing reps for the recruiters and former admissions counselors and advisors for the SSA positions.

SSAs are assigned students based on major or specialty. Each associate's load is about the same, depending upon the complexity of the major.

Steele admits there's been some turnover from the restructuring and acknowledges it's been difficult for some people who've come out of more traditional advising modes. "Some can't understand why they have to make calls rather than wait for the students to come in," she says. "Others have built a strong allegiance to their students."

The Process in Action

After acceptance, students are sent a profile of their SSA that includes the associate's personal mission, favorite quotes, and where they received their degree. There are also pictures of the individual SSAs on the wall in the center.

Steele explains that SSAs have become the eyes and ears of the institution. "They know whether the financial aid office is behind in processing and who the favorite faculty are."

To ensure their success, the university empowers SSAs to make decisions that, in the past, says Steele, had been made at higher levels. For example: SSAs can now waive a requirement, increase enrollment in a course, or adjust a bill.

The school overcame whatever resistance there was to the SSAs' increased decision-making ability by having them work with program directors — instructors who serve both as faculty and in an administrative capacity. With SSAs doing much of the mundane, day-to-day work, program directors can work with students at a higher level.

While SSAs can't do everything, their motto is "the buck stops here."

1995 Update

Editor's note: Linda Steele updates this article (below) with a description of the differences she sees between Franklin's program and other programs and the impact at Franklin.

Four aspects set Student Services apart from staff at other universities. *Ownership and empowerment* are the first. Dr. Paul J. Otte, University President, explains, "The buck stops with the SSAs — they own student problems and strive to solve them at every level. As a result, they have been empowered to make decisions such as substituting classes, course waivers, and awarding transfer credit. Decisions formerly requiring faculty, departmental, or dean authorization can now be made by the SSA."

Secondly, they provide *consistency*. The same SSA works with a student from admission through graduation. Students are encouraged to work with their SSA immediately, to begin developing a personal plan for their course work at Franklin.

A third principle involves the university moving from prescriptive advising on a trimester-to-trimester basis to *developmental advising* — a long-term goal setting and planning strategy.

Finally, the university can now internally *project and monitor student enrollment*. SSAs, in consultation with academic program administrators, identify enrollment goals with their portfolio students.

The process of implementing this new philosophy required delicate handling and attention to human resource management. Training activities included working with the academic departments in order to set parameters for decision-making, team-building exercises, and periodic motivational programs. The university coordinated an internal marketing campaign focused on the SSAs as part of the planned activities during an Opening Week Celebration. Posing the question, "Do you know your Student Services Associate?" provided an opportunity to promote the program in an unassuming manner while compelling students to identify their personal SSA.

Continuous program evaluation is based on the success of improved services to students, enhanced relationships with students, and attainment of enrollment goals. For example, the number of students using the university's streamlined registration process through telephone, fax, or mail-ins increased from 464 students in 1992 to 1,282 students in 1993. The university's new emergency loan program has assisted 21 students with over $8,000, and the deferred payment program impacted 300 students in 1992 and 700 students in 1993. The projected enrollment increase was exceeded. In 1993-94, one year after implementation of the program, the university generated an additional $420,277 worth of tuition revenues, as compared with 1992-93. This represents a 3.7% increase in credit hours, a 7.6% increase in new students, and a 2.2% increase in overall students.

Relationship management has proven to have widespread institutional impact. Colleges and universities around the country that are concerned with improved student services, increased enrollment, and improved retention can learn from the Franklin University model and adopt a relationship management philosophy at their institution.

For more information, contact:

Linda Steele, Vice President for Students, Franklin University, 201 S. Grant, Columbus, OH 43215; Ph: 614/341-6230. (October 1993)

Schools Cut Recruitment Costs

By revising the way they provide information to prospective and current students, the University of Pittsburgh has reduced recruitment and retention costs.

Traditionally, each December the University of Pittsburgh mails a financial aid packet to all current students. Until recently, the packet contained an aid renewal application, instructions, an application supplement, and an FAF. Since the renewal application contains personal information, such as the student's Social Security number and citizenship, postal regulations require that the packets be mailed first class.

The school cut its mailing costs in half by splitting the packet into two mailings: one first class and one bulk. The first class mailing includes the renewal application and a card stating that the other materials are being mailed under separate cover. The rest is bulk mailed a week later. The split mailing saves the University of Pittsburgh $4,000 annually.

For more information, contact:

Betsy Porter, Director of Admissions and Financial Aid, University of Pittsburgh, Pittsburgh, PA 15260-0001; Ph: 412/624-7164. (July 1991)

Chicago State University: Recruitment and Retention Begin at the Top

When Dolores Cross took over the presidency of Chicago State University in August 1990, the university was retaining approximately half of its first-year students. And just 20% of the students were completing their degrees within seven years.

Since then, Cross's dual goals of boosting enrollment and retention are bearing fruit. Her efforts, together with those of many motivated CSU faculty and staff, led to a fall 1994 enrollment increase of 68% over 1989 figures — the highest increase of any Illinois state school.

Communication and Commitment Are the Keys

To what does she attribute these successes? Communication. "You need to create a caring environment and be attentive to the interaction between faculty and students," she explains. She believes in spreading the college's message to all constituencies — faculty, staff, students, community. And it works.

The college, located in an urban area 12 miles south of the Chicago Loop, attracts 98% of its students from Illinois. Nearly 90% of CSU's 10,000 students are minorities. Women compose 68% of the student body. The average age of a CSU undergraduate — many of whom are first generation — is 27.

Cross's first efforts focused on recruitment. In July, just before she arrived, the faculty had volunteered to call all accepted applicants. "They [faculty] had just completed strategic planning workshops and knew the enrollment realities," she explains.

During the phonathon, over 2,500 applicants received personal phone calls from 90 faculty, student affairs staff, and Cross herself. Not only did the calls contribute to an overall increase of 18%, officials noted a 25% increase in day students. A side benefit: CSU discovered that the academic profile of the incoming class rose. "The calls showed the students that someone cares," Cross explains.

The next step was establishing new retention goals. For help, Cross turned to the faculty and academic departments. "We've said the responsibility for improving the success of students is at the department level," she stresses. "Whether or not students persist is an academic issue. It's not something that can be relegated solely to student services."

Cross invited faculty to submit proposals to help achieve these increased retention goals. As encouragement, she made available $75,000 in incentive funds.

Out of 264 faculty, 104 submitted proposals. The 25 projects that received funding included a math hotline for homework, several projects using peer tutors, and an idea to team faculty and students for physics research. "Rather than mandating from the top," says Cross, "the faculty came up with their own solutions."

Cross also assessed each university department 1% of its budget to establish an office of academic support services. The office monitors students, tracking them down if they don't show up for class. It offers tutoring, counseling, and mentoring "so students don't get lost." In addition to establishing the office, Cross also implemented a peer tutoring program, expanded library hours, and reduced class sizes. The results have been dramatic. One-year retention increased from 55% to 66% and two-year retention climbed from 35% to 50%.

Focus Groups Assess the Campus Climate

To help assess the campus climate, Cross hired a consultant to conduct separate focus groups for faculty and students. She explains, "I wanted to see how both groups experience the environment at CSU."

Cross distributed the results in a series of 10, two-hour faculty workshops. The "Communication Clarification" workshops give Cross a chance to clarify her message and get faculty feedback without administrative filtering. "It's basically, 'This is what I'm saying. Do you understand? Do you have questions?' " explains Cross.

For her efforts, Cross has received enthusiastic support. But she also understands the need to temper enthusiasm to prevent burnout.

"Many have gone beyond the conventional and are performing heroic acts," she stresses.

Concern about faculty burnout led her to adopt a volunteer-staffed mentoring program. "You need to increase the core of people who are there for the students," she explains. Now, 60 volunteers from the community — including the retired superintendent of police — help convey a caring atmosphere.

Cross is a firm believer in the power of communication. Fall and spring convocations educate faculty about the actions that emanate from strategic planning sessions and research. Area parents receive a "Consumer Report" talking about the changes at CSU. Open house retreats for civil service workers, faculty, and students offer her feedback on the changes. "I have a sense of the realities they're experiencing," she says.

Now that she sees progress toward her recruitment and retention goals, Cross is looking at future challenges. But students are her first priority. "You have a moral responsibility to be responsive to the students who have so many concerns vying for their attention," she explains. "CSU students are underprepared but have potential and the desire to succeed. My goal is to provide safety nets, yet at the same time keep a quality program."

For more information, contact:

Dolores Cross, President, Chicago State University, 95th St. at King Dr., Chicago, IL 60628; Ph: 312/995-2400. (July 1991)

Students Take Five and Broaden their Horizons

Degree requirements prevent many students from exploring other avenues of interest. But at the University of Rochester (NY), those who are intellectually curious and adventurous can "Take Five" and spend a tuition-free, fifth year enhancing their education.

William Green, dean of undergraduate studies, explains that Take Five maximizes a student's chance to get a liberal education. "It's a very individually centered program," he remarks. "Take Five celebrates self-awareness, self-discovery, and the individual differences among students." On the practical side, it also gives students a lot more freedom in planning their fourth and fifth years.

Students can apply to the program as soon as they've chosen their major, but no later than the second semester of their junior year.

The application process itself is a learning experience. Applicants have to write an essay that discusses their educational and academic goals and how the extra courses they've selected will help them reach those goals. "The whole application process is an opportunity for students to explain to themselves and to us how they've planned their education," says Green. "Students have to make a case for the fifth year; they get to tell us what's central in their interests and how they intend to enrich their education." A committee selects the most compelling applications for the extra year.

Not everyone who applies is automatically granted a fifth year. Take Five isn't an entitlement, an excuse to do a double degree, or a remedial option. Although there are no GPA requirements, one of the very few guidelines is that the student must be able to finish his or her degree in four years. "It was never our intention to be a last-minute, spur-of-the-moment thing," Green says. "Take Five was conceived solely as an enrichment program — to fill out or to balance the degree requirements."

A snapshot of two recent Take Five graduates suggests some of the possibilities. One, a double major in history and Chinese, spent the extra year taking psychology and biology classes to deepen her awareness of the makeup of individuals. The other, an optical engineering major with a minor in studio arts and a management studies certificate, used her year to take additional art courses as well as voice lessons. She combined her background in optics with her artistic skills to create a set of holograms for an art show.

Originally developed in 1986 with a more structured set of requirements and an enrollment cap, Take Five is now open to anyone with a good proposal. Green notes that what Take Five students give back to the college is well worth the cost of their courses. "They bring a maturity, a kind of perspective, an ease about their learning. They know themselves and their goals well."

For more information, contact:

William Green, Dean of Undergraduate Studies, University of Rochester, Rochester, NY 14627; Ph: 716/275-2351. (February 1992)

Improving Productivity through Performance Management

In 1987, Western Michigan University's admissions office faced a six-week turnaround time on applications and a backlog of some 2,000 credit evaluations. The office was also experiencing high overtime costs, high absenteeism among the processing staff, and low morale.

Since then, the office has cut its turnaround time to under two weeks during peak months (four days during non-peak months) and, for the last three years, reduced annual overtime costs to zero from an original high of over $10,000. The secret: Performance Management (PM).

Performance Management emphasizes regular positive and corrective feedback to improve productivity and quality of work life.

How did PM come to WMU? Leslie Wilk, a consultant at the Center for Entrepreneurial Studies and Development at West Virginia University, explained: "While working on my master's in industrial psych at WMU, I was also a graduate assistant in the tour office — next to the copy machine. ... I overheard a lot of complaints about the processing of admissions applications. Since my education was teaching me to solve these types of problems, I knew I could do something about them." Wilk began to analyze the system and evaluate means by which to change the structure.

Wilk first introduced a system to measure the work each employee was completing each day. At her suggestion, the office had another graduate student check the system's validity and accuracy.

Congratulations, You're Hired! And by the Way ...

Just as WMU was implementing PM, Pamela Liberacki was hired to supervise the processing staff. Wilk trained her in the PM concepts.

Liberacki recalls her start. "Initially, I wasn't crazy about PM because it [the system] was all put in place before I started . ... Actually," she adds, "you could say I was a bit resistive."

But she tried it. She reviewed with each employee the previous day's work and set new goals, specifying the amount and type of work to do. Then, twice a day she provided brief positive feedback. If a worker was engaging in an unrelated activity (typing labels rather than loading applications), Liberacki would redirect him or her with corrective feedback.

Initially there was employee resistance to being monitored. Wilk recalled absenteeism maxed out during the first week of the program. "Some attitudes were: if I don't show up, it will go away," said Wilk.

But results soon overcame skepticism. The most dramatic increase in productivity came in application processing. Before PM, one processor loaded a weekly average of 22 applications; that average rose to 185. Credit evaluators boosted their weekly average of 175 reviews to 380. The results increased enthusiasm. Gradually, Liberacki reduced her involvement; the staff became more self-sustaining — and reported greater satisfaction and better morale.

With such success in the processing area, the director of admissions and orientation, Stanley Henderson, was eager to implement PM with the counselors. So he had his other associate director design her program to include weekly, half-hour one-on-one meetings with each staff member. During these meetings, staff used PM cards listing tasks and accomplishments as a basis for discussion.

Since the meetings provided structured feedback and discussion, counselors reported greater job satisfaction and supervisor support — and interrupted their supervisor less often during non-meeting times, leading to greater productivity for counselors and supervisors.

Then both administrators asked Henderson to design PM plans for their own positions. They kept daily logs on tasks and accomplishments, and Henderson scheduled semi-monthly individual meetings with them and semi-monthly strategic planning and evaluation meetings as a group. All three administrators reported better communications and a clearer understanding of their environment.

Wilk warned that supervisors must offer feedback sincerely. She also calls administrative support essential. "It's important that ... leaders model behaviors desired in lower levels of the organization."

Liberacki is now sold on PM. "It's a workable, positive, exciting venture. Ultimately, it did as much for me as it did for my staff."

For more information, contact:

Pamela Liberacki, Associate Director for Support Services, Western Michigan University, Kalamazoo, MI 49008; Ph: 616/387-2000 or Center for Entrepreneurial Studies and Development, Inc., College of Engineering, P.O. Box 6101, West Virginia University, Morgantown, WV 26506; Ph: 304/293-5551. (December 1991)

San Juan College Thinks 'Culture' When Recruiting Native Americans

Wanting to refine its recruitment efforts, San Juan College (NM) decided to call in a consultant. When he suggested direct mail, telemarketing, and home visits, Donna Ogilvie, San Juan's public information officer, interrupted. "Those kinds of techniques may work with most students, but not with our Native American population."

The two-year college is adjacent to the 150,000-member Navajo Reservation, largest in the country. About 28% of San Juan's student body are Native Americans. While the majority of this group is Navajo, the school also enrolls members of 12 other tribes.

Many proven recruitment efforts don't work here, Ogilvie explains. "The homes are miles apart, and the majority don't have phones or mailboxes." What does work, the college has found, is recruitment strategies that incorporate an under-standing of Navajo culture.

San Juan recruits extensively on the Navajo reservation. Admissions staff visit regional junior and senior high schools, encouraging students to visit the campus. Booths at tribal fairs and informational exhibits in shopping centers, community chapters, and trading posts, as well as parade floats, contribute to an increased awareness of the college among tribal members.

The college understands and effectively uses the Navajo's respect for their elders. "The elders are the decision-makers," says Freda Garnanez, director of San Juan's Native American program. Two of the seven members of the Board of Trustees are Navajo who live on the reservation and regularly help with recruitment.

Judicious use of the Navajo language is also key to recruitment. The college circulates a four-minute video narrated in Navajo to all of the chapter houses (government structures on the reservation). Announcements on a local television keep the college in the forefront. The college even offers the Navajo language and Navajo history in courses.

College Makes Dreams Possible

San Juan succeeds not by implementing especially innovative recruitment techniques, but by adapting traditional techniques to reservation life and using recruitment strategies that harmonize with tribal culture. For example, the Possible Dream scholarship program encourages all eighth-graders — not only Native Americans — to consider college. And it provides funding for two years of tuition.

The students — or their families — pay $10 per month for five years until they finish 12th grade. After five years, with accrued interest and a $125 scholarship from the sponsor (U S West), the students have enough funds to attend San Juan for two full years.

Tuition is guaranteed, regardless of increases. If students fail to complete the program, all the money is returned, less a $25 bookkeeping fee. "It's been a highly successful program," notes Ogilvie. "About 125 students sign up each year."

Throughout the program, the students receive regular mailings from San Juan, personal visits from a counselor, and an invitation to an annual summer social held at the college. In August 1994, the first class of Possible Dream Scholars began at San Juan.

Culture and Retention

San Juan works as hard at retaining the students as it does recruiting them. Faculty and administrators are sensitive to the Native American cultures and attitudes.

For example, they've discovered that their priorities aren't necessarily priorities for many Native Americans. Some students are not concerned with setting priorities in preparation for college. The submission of various documents required for college entrance and financial aid is not done until it is time for the semester to begin. But for administrators, such documents as applications and transcripts have to be on file before a student can be fully accepted to the college.

Time isn't of the essence to Native Americans. As long as there is time in a day, there is time to do things.

The faculty also learns to appreciate Native American beliefs and not penalize students who refuse to participate in activities. Ogilvie relates an incident where a Navajo student refused to dissect anything in a biology class. "That student believed that the spirit of the animal would be disturbed if he did so."

The college has a strong Native American support program which includes advising and counseling services for all Indian students. The Indian Club hosts an annual powwow that attracts tribal members from throughout the country.

The lessons of San Juan College are applicable to recruiting not only Native Americans but members of all special groups.

For more information, contact:

Freda Garnanez, Director of the Native American Program, San Juan College, 4601 College Blvd., Farmington, NM 87401-4699; Ph: 505/599-0321. (April 1994)

Ohio State University Works to Attract Minority Graduate Students

Between 1982 and 1992, the number of minority students in graduate and professional schools grew by nearly 79% while white enrollments increased only 19%. Yet the numbers of minority graduate students are still small. Ohio State University addresses the problem of low numbers with a comprehensive group of programs designed to support the special needs of the minority student.

OSU recognized early on its responsibility to increase the diversity of the graduate school. "Graduate school is the search for truth and the exploration of ideas," says Jean Dickerscheid, associate dean of the graduate school. "And you can't do that from a WASP perspective."

Ohio State's Plan of Attack

Increase Numbers of Prospective Students

The most important initiative that graduate and professional schools can take to increase minority enrollment is to cultivate and enlarge the pool of potential students. OSU does this by participating in several minority name exchange programs, including the Committee for Institutional Cooperation (CIC) and National Name Exchanges, as well as the GRE Minority Locator Service. Through the exchanges, each participating university supplies the other consortium members with information on minority juniors and seniors interested in attending graduate school. "We contact the undergraduates and ask if they would like to participate," Dickerscheid explains. "It's strictly voluntary." Students who agree fill out a biographical sheet. The information is compiled and sent to the other institutions.

When OSU receives the lists, it distributes them to the individual departments and programs. "Each identified student is sent appropriate literature and invited to apply," adds Dickerscheid.

Is the graduate school concerned about competing for OSU students whose names are listed with the exchanges? "We're more concerned that they go on to graduate school. Attending a different school gives those students a different perspective on their discipline, as well as enlarging academic connections. We encourage them to do at least one of their advanced degrees elsewhere."

Fund Departmental Recruitment

Most of OSU's recruitment efforts focus on the reputation of the faculty and the department as well as on the financing available. Rather than going out and doing any specific recruiting, the graduate school supports the programs and efforts of individual departments. Through a competition open to all graduate programs, the "Recruitment Grant Program" supports departmental recruitment of students, with an emphasis on minorities. Awards of up to $1,000 are available to departments to assist them in recruiting minorities.

Set Up Visitation Programs

Special visitation programs encourage prospective minority students to view the campus — helping them determine if OSU is a good match for them. The "Campus Visitation Program" provides travel funds for fellowship nominees. The "Graduate and Professional Schools Visitation Days" annually bring to campus some 300 minority students from 60 historically black institutions and 10 institutions with large Hispanic enrollments. OSU pays the cost of transportation, hotels, and most meals, so there's little or no cost to the students.

Offer Strategy Workshops

Representatives from graduate programs improve their recruiting efforts by participating in strategy workshops which offer a special emphasis on the recruitment of minorities. Instructions on using a prospective student database, suggestions from departments with good track records in minority recruitment, and a guest speaker from Educational Testing Service are examples of recent workshops.

Provide Summer Research Opportunities

For the "Summer Research Opportunities Program" (SROP), undergraduate minority students are selected through a competition to work on a research project with a faculty mentor during a summer quarter between their sophomore and junior years. To be eligible, students must be in good standing, with at least a 2.75 GPA. Nearly 500 students have benefited from this program since its inception ten years ago.

Currently integrated into SROP is an internship program with historically black colleges. "Seven students from other schools worked on projects with faculty mentors last summer," notes Dickerscheid.

Solicit Alumni Feedback

An alumni council composed of representatives from business, government and industry as well as academics advises the dean of the graduate school on recruitment and retention strategies as well as on other matters. "Despite being relatively new, the council already has a success story," states Dickerscheid. "One alumnus worked out a fellowship program at his firm that included summer internships and a promise of future employment for a minority student, and another gave money for a minority fellowship."

Revamp Publications

The graduate school administrators at OSU reconceptualized and redesigned the graduate school bulletin to make it more effective as a recruiting tool. "We wanted to display all of the rich resources of the university," says Dickerscheid. "We included a PR portion that contains campus and community shots and followed that with an outline of the programs we offer. And since students are attracted to schools based on department reputation, we listed all the names, specializations and degrees of the 3,000 graduate faculty."

Award Fellowships

The graduate school offers a number of fellowships to new minority students in their first year of studies toward a master's or Ph.D. degree, with a stipend of approximately $11,400 and a tuition authorization. Among the fellowships are "Special University Fellowships," awarded to students who need to complete undergraduate prerequisites before starting graduate coursework, who are graduates of little-known institutions, or who received low scores on qualifying exams.

In addition to the above campus-based programs, OSU also participates in "Project 1000," a national effort to recruit Hispanics.

Ohio State recognizes that today's graduate and professional students are tomorrow's leaders, academicians, and role models. By working to increase the numbers of minorities enrolled in graduate school, the university strives to improve minority participation in society.

For more information, contact:

Jean D. Dickerscheid, Associate Dean of the Graduate School, 250 University Hall, 230 N. Oval Mall, The Ohio State University, Columbus, OH 43210; Ph: 614/292-6031. (April 1990)

Faculty/Admissions Office Partnership Changes Recruiting Focus

by Jennifer Lind

The name says it all: "Creative Departmental Marketing." The descriptively titled program unites faculty at Salem State College (MA) with potential students.

Director of Admissions David Sartwell lists two positive elements — faculty knowledge of programs and faculty acquaintanceship with individuals outside of the college community — and one negative element — falling application numbers at the 12,000-student college — as his reasons for starting the program in 1988.

"I couldn't do all this by myself," says Sartwell. "There are too many high schools. There were important questions that only faculty members could answer. With this program, we get faculty and people from outside the campus to help bring in students. Those are the connections we need to make this work. It's a tremendous number of cross linkages."

Twelve departments are currently involved in the program, ranging from theatre and art to business and geography. The differences between these departments would seem to discourage equal success, but Sartwell says that isn't the case. Each works off a simple template or goal: "recognize the characteristics of each department, maximize the good people who are doing things, and match them with people outside to establish a networking system."

Faculty response to this outreach has mainly been positive, says Sartwell. "Of course, it (the motivation to volunteer) depends on the individual. Some view recruiting as someone else's job. Some are more naturally outgoing. Our mission is to find faculty in the departments who would enjoy recruiting. Then, [our goal is] finding members in that field outside the university who understand you have excellent programs in the school."

The School of Nursing was the first targeted in 1988. Diane Lapkin, Dean of the School of Human Services, credits the program with motivating faculty to recruit students. "When I first came aboard, some professors' programs were very low in the number of those enrolled." she explains. "Some professors were afraid of their programs being cut."

Instead of recruiting solely from high schools, the school branched out into the community. Admissions counselors and volunteering faculty members held brunches in a local hospital for potential students, for example.

Partly because of the recruiting program, and partly because of a general trend toward more nursing applicants, the school's enrollment levels increased substantially from 670 in 1991 to 1377 in 1993, says Lapkin.

The nursing program became a model for the rest of the college, she adds. "It changed the focus of recruiting. The faculty and admissions office worked in more of a partnership; the professors bring knowledge about their field, while guidance counselors bring knowledge about the market," says Lapkin.

Along with collaborating with professionals outside the college, faculty are involved in job fairs, educational fairs, and high school visits.

In one case, students from about 30 high schools from the area will attend the theatre department for a day. They're able to choose three out of five workshops, meet professors, and get a taste of campus life, says Sartwell. "We teamed the theatre faculty with theatre people from the high schools," he explains. "It isn't a complicated idea, but it does take some time to do."

This in-house approach may aid other schools suffering from declining enrollment. The program costs between $6,000 and $8,000 per year. "That's paying for kids' lunches, some mileage. It isn't a high-cost program. We stay away from flash and dance," says Sartwell.

The main success, says Lapkin, is faculty members "have seen that it's very successful to work as a partner with the admissions office. We can share resources and knowledge in a low-cost way. That's what we've learned from this approach."

For more information, contact:

David Sartwell, Director of Admissions, Admissions Office, or Diane Lapkin, Dean of the Schools of Human Services, Salem State College, 352 Lafayette St., Salem, MA 01915; Ph: 508/741-6200 (Sartwell) or 741-6630 (Lapkin). (April 1994)

Employees Get on the Line for Triton College

It's often difficult to encourage employees not directly involved in recruitment and retention to support those efforts. Yet as more schools adopt the attitude that shaping enrollment is an institutional responsibility, a movement is underway to redefine the roles of all college staff — from president to maintenance worker — as influencers of recruitment and retention.

Persuading faculty and staff to assume a role in an area where they might not feel comfortable isn't easy. But Triton College (IL) — a community college — convinced its employees to assist in recruitment and retention efforts through employee-sponsored, large-scale telethons called "Triton's On The Line." "During the past five years more than 75 faculty and staff have participated in a telethon," says Gwen Kanelos, Dean of Student Services.

Why did Triton undertake such a project? A brief profile of the college's market will help clarify its decision.

The school draws much of its enrollment from the near western suburbs of Chicago. That district is aging, with few young families moving in. "This necessitates an intensive marketing plan, in which personal contact plays a key role," explains Kanelos. The telethons began in 1989 as a result of an attempt to align many of the institution's recruiting activities with retention and involve the campus community in the process. "We needed to expand the telephone campaigns that were previously coordinated and staffed solely by the admissions office," says Kanelos.

She adds, "The telethons give us additional staff at little or no cost. In addition, employees gain a new understanding of what it takes to recruit and retain students. They have more of an appreciation for what the admission staff do."

The logistics of the telephone campaigns are simple. Triton conducts six telethons per year, three every semester, with each running for three days at a time — Tuesday, Wednesday, and Thursday. The time commitment is reasonable — only two and a half hours — from 5:00 to 7:30 p.m. Prior to each session, 10-12 volunteers receive training — conducted over dinner — before they make the calls. Volunteers work from a script, and an enrollment management staff member remains "on-duty" each evening of the telethon to answer questions.

Although Triton's telethons are fairly standard, what makes them atypical is the composition of the volunteers. The school divides its volunteers into five groups: faculty, mid-managers, administrators, full-time classified/clerical, and current students. Any employee group or the student government may sponsor a campaign. Sponsorship entails recruiting volunteers from the targeted group, recommending refreshments, selecting a leader, and identifying the group on any printed materials.

To promote the telethons and help recruit additional participants, each volunteer receives a small recognition gift, imprinted with the "Triton's On The Line" logo. The items are underwritten with funds from student association.

The telethons have proven effective — both in generating enrollments and promoting positive public relations. During one telethon, employees attempted 1800 calls to currently enrolled students who hadn't re-enrolled for the next semester. The results revealed that the most common response to the call was an expression of appreciation. Many people indicated that they had simply forgotten to register and were grateful for the reminder."

Another telethon reached nearly 1100 prospective students — 46% of whom said they planned to enroll at Triton. An additional 30% were unsure about enrolling but seemed positive about the call.

These telethons supplement the regular, ongoing personal calls to prospective and current students by the admission staff. On the average, each telethon attempts to contact specific groups of 600 to 3000 students, such as those who didn't re-enroll, orientation no-shows, or applicants who haven't registered for classes.

The telethons have reaped tremendous benefits for Triton College. "As a result of this inclusive program, we are able to reach a greater number of students in a shorter period of time. In addition, we're able to implement more personalized outreach techniques and quickly determine which factors influence nonenrollment," says Kanelos.

"Most importantly," she says, "telethon participation lets staff know how influential they are. It increases their understanding of recruitment and retention efforts and the importance of this being an institutional responsibility."

For more information, contact:

Gwen E. Kanelos, Dean of Student Services, Triton College, 2000 Fifth Ave., River Grove,IL 60171; Ph: 708/456-0300, ext 3815. (August 1990)

The Proof Is in the Advertising

Pardon Iona College (NY) if it toots its own horn. For each of the past six years, the college has experienced a 10%-20% rise in admission applications, thanks to an advertising campaign. Even more remarkable, it's accomplished this in a region that at the same time experienced an annual decline of 14%-18% among traditional-aged students.

In the mid-'80s, when Iona officials began reading the demographic handwriting on the wall, they decided to hire a full-service advertising agency to build the college's image and improve awareness among area high school students, parents, alumni, corporate recruiters, and friends. They chose CDHM Advertising (CT), a firm with no other higher education clients, because, they felt it had the ability to position their institution and services.

Before venturing into advertising, Iona had relied on traditional recruitment methods: direct mail and sporadic newspaper ads. There was no central theme tying these efforts together.

Creating an Image

CDHM began by researching Iona's strengths and weaknesses. That research revealed that the biggest negative was the lack of image for the college. The agency translated the study's findings into a comprehensive positioning/communications theme, "Iona College: The Proof is in the People," which was used initially on all of the college's printed material.

Using that theme, the college reduced its reliance on newspaper ads and shifted its focus, based on CDHM's research, to radio and TV. Convincing people of the advantages of broadcast media — particularly TV — was a hard-fought battle. Several trustees who held positions in advertising helped gain approval for TV ads.

Once the campaign began, the effects were immediate and quite positive throughout the target audiences. For example, by converting Iona's graduate programs from newspaper advertising to radio, the college saw a 45% increase in enrollment in 1991.

And the campaign's impact wasn't felt only in the admissions office. Alumni reaction resulted in an upswing in annual giving despite a recession market.

Joseph Del Galdo, president of CDHM, acknowledges that most schools are afraid to use an ad agency. "They don't understand what ... we do and they're afraid it will cost a lot of money. Actually, we generally save money for the client because advertising pays for its own costs out of efficiencies. And agencies receive some of their compensation directly from the media.

"One of the benefits of having one organization or person in charge," says Del Galdo, "is that all of the advertising has a cohesive look so it builds over the years." Another benefit is that, since they were no longer judging their own work, the typical problems of politics and pride of authorship didn't get in the way.

Besides impacting enrollment and alumni giving, the campaign garnered Iona 11 national and regional marketing awards.

For those concerned about the cost of using an advertising agency, Iona College offers this advice: Look carefully at what you're already doing and find out where you can pull money without endangering anything. Start on a small scale and then build. And remember: nothing gets you more money in a budget like success.

For more information, contact:

Jennifer Doherty, Director of Advertising and Publications, Iona College, New Rochelle, NY 10801; Ph: 914/633-2000; or Joseph Del Galdo, President, CDHM Advertising, 750 E. Main, Stamford, CT 06902; Ph: 203/967-7200. (October 1992)

Original Marketing Helps Saint Vincent College Meet Its Goals

Eleven years ago, Saint Vincent College (PA), an all-male, Catholic, liberal arts institution, made the decision to admit women. At that time, the college's board of directors challenged the administration to find ways of increasing the percentage of women to 50% within five years. The college attained its goal in four years — attributing its success, in part, to some rather unique marketing techniques.

One of the more original efforts occurred several years ago when officials decided to capitalize on Saint Vincent's location — directly across the road from an airport. "We purchased mailing lists of families with pilots' licenses, advertised in plane publications and even developed posters to hang in airports," says Don Orlando, director of public relations. A 'fly-in' visitation program brought 40 students to campus, six of whom decided to enroll.

Although the college experienced moderate success with its flight connections, officials decided not to actively pursue them. But because of the positive relationship developed between the college and local airport officials, the U.S. Navy Thunderbirds — in town for an air show that spring — did a wing-tip salute over Saint Vincent immediately after the commencement ceremony.

One addition to the marketing plan was a full-page display advertisement in *Reader's Digest*. "We chose *Reader's Digest* for several reasons," explains Orlando. "The publication has a pretty good life span and reaches a large marketing area. We wanted to target parents and let them know we're a high-quality college so the ad was designed as an 'image enhancer' rather than a clip coupon."

After developing the ad, the college experienced a 12% rise in applications in January 1989 and another 16% increase in January 1990. And they've received lots of comments about it.

"While we've had a healthy and stable enrollment for many years," says Orlando, "we're not content to rest on our laurels. In addition to the traditional methods of advertising, telemarketing and direct mail, we try various things each year to explore new markets or test new techniques."

Orlando attributes the college's success to a president who encourages things to happen quickly without unnecessary 'bureaucratic decision-making.' "He allows creativity to prosper and mistakes to be made. And he builds flexibility into the budget to allow us to test things."

For more information, contact:

Don Orlando, Director of Public Relations, Saint Vincent College, Latrobe, PA 15650-2690; Ph: 412/537-4560. (April 1990)

Key Steps in Working Successfully with Alumni Volunteers

Alumni volunteers need to be supported, nurtured, and recognized. They also need a job description and goals. According to James McCoy, Associate Vice President of Enrollment at Miami University, there are two crucial points to consider before setting up an alumni volunteer program:

- What should these volunteers accomplish?

- What will the start-up *and* long-range costs be?

As part of the development of the alumni admissions program at Miami University, McCoy has compiled a step-by-step plan for building a successful alumni volunteer team.

Step 1: Assess Institutional Needs.

Is using alumni appropriate in terms of your goals? What will these alumni do, and how will they do it? These questions must be answered if volunteers are to be successful.

Step 2: Set Goals for Volunteer Involvement.

Volunteers are successful when perceived as *partners*. Since lack of time will be the largest stumbling block for them, it's important that goals be clear and support the central mission of the institution.

Step 3: Establish Resources and Funding for Support.

Volunteers aren't free. They *must* be supported through staff time and material. Make sure the appropriate level of resources are available before you talk to your first alumni.

Step 4: Identify and Recruit Volunteers.

Recruiting volunteers is the job of those running the program. Know what type of individuals are needed and why they should be involved. Be ready with a program *before* you recruit.

Step 5: Assign Activities Based on a Planning Calendar.

Use a regular calendar, rather than an academic calendar, to plan activities. Plan 18 months ahead. Set up each event by month and cross-reference by activity for that month. Develop an activity grid detailing duties for the admissions professional, committee leader, and volunteers, and share the grid with the volunteers.

Step 6: Set Success Parameters Based on Identified Outcomes.

Set specific targets — and recognize those who reach their goals.

Step 7: Establish an Information Exchange Mechanism.

An information exchange by telephone, newsletter, or computer hook-up is a *must* for volunteers to represent the institution effectively. They need to be told how a message should be presented and why. This involves a complete training program.

Step 8: Gather Outcomes and Maintain Records.
Formulate a cost/benefit ratio for your academic promotional efforts and keep accurate records to analyze the benefits of your volunteers.

Step 9: Evaluate the Degree of Success.
Develop an evaluation model before you begin. A yearly evaluation will determine if you've met your goals within the budget.

Step 10: Revamp Goals and Resources Based on Bottom-Line Evaluation.
Continually upgrade your program. Revamp, delete, or replace goals to keep the program targeted toward tomorrow's needs.

For more information, contact:

James McCoy, Associate Vice President of Enrollment, Miami University, Oxford, OH 45056.

Collaboration Makes Transfers "Supergraduates"

Much attention is focused on students whose academic skills lie at extremes on the spectrum. Colleges court high-ability students with offers of full-tuition scholarships. Students whose academic efforts fall short of success become the subjects of studies and remedial programs.

In the middle lie the average students — students whose grades and test scores won't attract attention from many schools but who have the potential for success. Fortunately, some institutions are developing programs to tap into that potential. West Los Angeles College (WLAC), in cooperation with Hamilton High School and UCLA, recently launched a pilot project to encourage average students to consider college.

Aptly termed the "Supergraduate" program, this collaboration targets B- and C+ students from underrepresented groups — such as minorities or low-income — who have the potential to succeed in higher education but who may not be motivated or prepared to do so. They take the middle-of-the-road students, the ones who, given strengthening-type experiences and support, could set goals in high school to go on to college and receive a four-year degree.

Two factors influenced the program's development. The first was the "Transfer Alliance," a partnership between 10 Los Angeles area community colleges and the College of Letters and Science at UCLA. Students enrolled in Transfer Alliance courses at the community colleges are guaranteed priority for admission to UCLA. With the TA curriculum, the colleges designate classes that 'slice a little higher' to challenge the students. They're really honors-type classes exclusively for TA students.

The second factor involved an "adoption" program sponsored by the Los Angeles school district. Under the program, businesses and other organizations could sponsor or "adopt" a school. WLAC — an inner-city community college — chose Hamilton High School — an urban, music and humanities "magnet" institution that's over 83% minority.

These two factors, combined with administrative enthusiasm at both the high school and community college levels, led WLAC to adapt the basic features of the Transfer Alliance program for Hamilton High School students and create the Supergraduate program.

The Supergraduate application process is very selective. Students submit applications describing their academic goals, write an autobiographical essay, undergo an assessment of their skill levels in English, and participate in an interview that includes their parents. Parental involvement is one of the key factors in the program. They've developed a student-parent network that continuously notifies both students and parents about their academic progress and offers parents support techniques related to successful student academic achievement.

A committee of faculty from the three institutions evaluates the applicants according to specific guidelines. They identify students from specific cultural, racial, and social groups who have the potential to be adequately prepared for university-level work.

How the Program Works

Those selected to participate begin the program with an intensive course the summer before their junior year. As juniors, Supergraduate participants follow a college-prep track required for admission to UCLA. During "free" periods in their junior and senior years, they attend college courses taught by WLAC faculty members, offered at both Hamilton and the community college.

After completing the summer session that follows graduation, Supergraduate students will have earned at least 30 units of college credit. They enter WLAC with sophomore status. After a year at WLAC, they transfer to UCLA with "guaranteed priority admission" as juniors. Just one year out of high school, they're prepared to enter UCLA — and succeed.

In addition to the coursework, the Supergraduate program builds skills that enhance learning. Faculty integrate critical thinking, writing, research, and study skills into the subject matter.

Supergraduate students must maintain a B- (2.85) GPA each semester. Failure to maintain this level or an overall GPA of 2.5 or higher results in academic probation. Students who fail to end probation within two semesters are dismissed from the program.

To help them prepare for their role as college students, the program schedules campus visits to WLAC and UCLA and allows the participants access to sporting events and libraries on both campuses.

Of the 27 students accepted into the program last year, 24 will continue this fall. Even though not all the students stayed with the program, their increased self-esteem has rubbed off into other areas. These students believe they can do things that they couldn't before.

Funding for the pilot project came from a $14,000 grant from the Sears-Roebuck Foundation, through the AACJC's "Keep America Working" project. The money covered some administrators' salaries, honoraria for the faculty, and bus trips to WLAC and UCLA; it also bought books for the participants — a policy which has since been changed. Both Hamilton and WLAC now fund the program.

Because of the district's concurrent enrollment policy, there's no tuition charge for WLAC classes taught at Hamilton, giving the students the opportunity to take classes at either campus. The students are able to save a year's tuition on their education.

Much of the credit for the program's success is due to faculty commitment. It's really a faculty-based program: they determine the standards, who gets in, and what's offered. Without their dedication, there'd be no program.

For more information, contact:

Frances T. Leonard, Program Coordinator of the Supergraduate Program, West Los Angeles College, 4800 Freshman Dr., Culver City, CA 90230-3500; Ph: 310/287-4203. (August 1993)

College Quality: More Than a Ranking

Editor's note: The following article comes from a session presented at the 50th annual NACAC convention.

Every year since 1983, the month of October has brought a new round in the battle over college rankings. Once the smoke has cleared, the question still remains: "How do you measure college quality?"

Joseph Cuseo, a psychology professor at Marymount College (CA), has developed an alternative set of criteria for judging college quality, one based on a review of the research done by some of higher education's most prominent scholars.

Cuseo's interest in the topic stems from the fact that 90%-95% of Marymount's students transfer to other institutions. Students often ask him for his opinion of a college. In trying to answer their questions, he's discovered that none of the major institutional characteristics that the media currently use as ranking criteria bear any significant relationship to positive college outcomes — and some are even antithetical to student success.

His review of the research leads him to suggest the following criteria:

Institutional mission: clarity, consistency, and integrity.

"Colleges with a focused mission that's clearly and consistently communicated in their institutional publications and public announcements," says Cuseo, "are colleges that provide a clear sense of purpose and direction to all members of the college community and, most effectively, promote student involvement and persistence to graduation."

Students, he adds, should be cautious of what the Pew Charitable Trust calls "mission blur" — colleges that are trying to be too many things to too many people — and "mission drift" — colleges which were teaching and student-oriented and are now drifting toward research. "Be skeptical of claims of great researchers *and* great teachers," Cuseo says.

Quality of teaching.

Teaching is the major college experience that affects the satisfaction of students, yet in a study from the University of Pennsylvania, 37% of undergraduates reported dissatisfaction with teaching.

"We have a cruel irony here: teaching is so important, yet faculty get little preparation in graduate school to do it," says Cuseo. And faculty development budgets, he notes, are often the first things to get cut.

Gathering information on an institution's faculty recruitment and promotion policy is a way of finding out just how seriously the school takes teaching.

"There's a trend toward recruiting research stars with a promise of light teaching loads," says Cuseo. "This will eventually drive up costs and be reflected in higher tuition because the college will need to hire part-time or adjunct faculty to teach what the researchers won't."

Quality of academic advising.

The number one source of student dissatisfaction with college, says Cuseo, is poor advising. In many institutions, not only is advising unrewarded, but it's deteriorated into a perfunctory, bureaucratic, clerical task. Why is good advising important? Studies show that 50% of all college students are undecided and, of the 50% who've declared a major, half of those change them before graduation.

Quality institutions offer their students knowledgeable, accessible advisors who are able to show some relationship between the courses they have to take and their future careers.

Student support during key transitions: the first- and final-year experiences.

Although many studies show the impact of the first year on student success and persistence, the irony, says Cuseo, is that often these students are taught by the least experienced teachers and have the largest class sizes. "Thus," says Cuseo, "special attention and effective support for freshmen would be one key characteristic of a high-quality college." The final or senior year experience helps give some closure to the college experience — "it helps them transition out," explains Cuseo, "and proactively prepares them for the job experience."

Student/faculty contact outside of the classroom.

Hallway chats, faculty eating lunch or dinner with students, and faculty sponsorship of student clubs all contribute to student retention. Research shows that the frequency of those contacts positively affects students' academic achievement, progress toward graduation, and students' seeking of post-graduate opportunities.

Cuseo points to one institution — as an incentive for faculty to interact with students — that offers free coffee if faculty drink it in the student lounge. Prospective students should look for opportunities for faculty/student joint research, students and faculty eating together, faculty who come early to class and chat, and faculty willingness to meet with prospective students.

Quality of the curriculum.

Rather than a coherent overview, recently there's been a concern that general education has degenerated into a "smorgasbord" of courses, that courses have become fractured, and that faculty have become hyperspecialized. "No one gets a Ph.D. in general education. At some schools, it's underfunded, and it has the largest classes, the weakest teachers, and the highest faculty-to-student ratio."

Quality institutions offer a core curriculum, interdisciplinary courses, a connection between the student's major and career, internships and co-ops, and meaningful honors and study-abroad programs.

Quality of the co-curriculum.

Many studies show that student involvement in the co-curricular life of a campus leads to increased retention. For institutions concerned about the costs of co-curricular activities, "peer power" — students helping other students — keeps costs down and allows students to gain experience that enhances their future careers.

In reviewing the research, Cuseo discovered that studies showed virtually zero correlation between GPA and success on the job. However, several did show a high correlation between leadership experience while in college and career success.

Important quality indicators include co-curricular transcripts, educational programming in the residence halls, and opportunities for volunteerism and community service, which lower-division students can use as exploratory internships.

Quality of institutional assessment.

How does education impact students' learning and development? How does a college measure its impact on students?

With the trend toward accountability, such things as the length of time it takes to get a degree, retention rates, the existence of student satisfaction surveys, and tracking mechanisms aren't only markers of a quality institution, but contribute to institutional survival.

Many institutions rely on reputation in the outside community as a measure of assessment, says Cuseo, a measure Alexander Astin notes represents an egocentric view of quality.

Cuseo also cautions about reading too much into the retention rates of highly selective institutions. Besides attracting highly able and motivated students, students who are dissatisfied may be more willing to stay and tough it out at a "name" college simply because of the expectation that the "name" will open doors for them after graduation.

The bottom line? We need to replace misleading mass-media "measures" of college quality with institutional-assessment criteria that are well-grounded in higher educational research and scholarship on student outcomes.

For more information, contact:

Joseph Cuseo, Dept. of Psychology, Marymount College, 30800 Palos Verdes Dr. E., Rancho Palos Verdes, CA 90274; Ph: 310/377-5501. (November 1994)

Address Correction Requested: Personalizing Direct Mail

Each year, the U.S. Postal Service expedites the arrival of 80 billion pieces — 70 billion third class and 10 billion first class — of direct mail. That number includes higher education's lifeblood, the Search.

Three panelists in a session at the National Association of College Admission Counselors conference — Arthur Affleck, assistant to the chancellor for academic and student affairs for Pennsylvania's state system of higher education; Joan Isaac Mohr, vice president and dean of admissions at Quinnipiac College (CT); and William Royall, president of Royall and Co. (VA) — offered tips on how to get the most out of your direct mail pieces.

1. "Research before you Search," says Affleck. "Often Search mailings are based on hunches, ... but what you really need to have is empirical data to back up your decisions."

2. Mohr encourages you to "plan your plan" — begin by planning the mailing sequence. Don't wait for your responses to come back before you decide what gets sent out next. Decide what your response will be, what will happen after that, and what will be the time frame.

3. "Insist on accountability from everyone involved in your mailing process," says Royall.

4. Affleck suggests looking at how the principles of continuous quality improvement can enhance your direct mail effort. Applying a systematic process to your campaign helps you determine whether you should be making incremental or wholesale changes to your direct mail.

5. "Plan your direct mail piece," says Mohr. "Will it be a letter alone, a letter with a brochure, a window envelope, an oversized envelope?" Consider the students' ease in getting information from the piece.

6. "Get started early enough to allow yourself time to make strategy decisions based on the results of the previous year's Search," says Royall. "Make your schedules then — not when you're in the middle of a project."

7. "Focus on the essentials," says Affleck. In order of importance they are the list, timing, copy, art (remember, you're dealing with the MTV generation), and format (large, small, odd-sized.)

8. "Can you depend on those you're relying on to get the piece out?"asks Mohr. The best package in the world won't get a response unless it's in the mail.

9. Royall asks, "Are you wasting money by not eliminating duplicate names from your Search mailing list?" Not only costly, duplicates are potentially embarrassing. Do a merge/purge on all of your mailing list segments and get a report that you can personally review.

10. Don't wait to send information on financial aid, says Affleck."Here's a potentially priceless opportunity to begin a productive relationship with the student — and the parent — by making the financial aid understood early."

11. Mohr suggests calculating the cost per inquiry — total your expenses including purchasing the names, preparing and mailing the piece, receiving the responses, and mailing the follow-up — to see how effectively you're spending your dollars.

12. "Are you taking your best prospects for granted?" asks Royall. If you send the regular version of your Search letter to prospects already in your inquiry pool, it's the same as not recognizing an old friend and reintroducing yourself. Send them a special letter to show you remember and to remind them why they should continue to be interested.

13. Affleck suggests using a third-party endorsement — for example a well-known, well-placed alumnus. But don't let alums over-promise or embarrass the institution.

14. Mohr encourages you to try something new each year. Split your Search into longer vs. shorter letters. Perhaps include a letter alone in one, a letter and brochure in another. Find out what works best for you.

15. "Are you considering only one list source for your mailings?"asks Royall. NRCCUA offers special selects and a net name deal that can help you solve specific marketing challenges.

16. Advance review panels for new copy and concepts can be helpful, says Affleck. Use student focus groups or let some of your younger staff members react to the new piece.

17. "Have you considered using direct mail to generate interest from overseas?" asks Mohr. If you decide to do so, use a third party to send the mailing — TNT, DHL, etc. — and be careful not to use the business reply stamp which doesn't work outside of the U.S.

18. Royall points out that the University Postal Service can be your best friend when trying to save money. There are substantial cost-reduction advantages to using ZIP + 4 and barcoding on your envelopes.

19. Imitation may be the sincerest form of flattery, but be careful that what you're copying is successful and will work for your institution. Affleck suggests copying concepts, not plagiarizing.

20. "Make something happen as a result of reading your appeal," says Mohr. Readers must be asked to *do* something — for example, send back a reply card to get a viewbook.

21. "Do you make your prospects an offer they can't refuse?" asks Royall. In any mailing that generates leads, 40% of the pulling power lies in the offer, 40% in the list, and 10% each in the art and the copy.

22. Affleck suggests that you repeat your request for a reply in several places. "The function of a direct mail piece is to get that first response — not to get them to enroll."

23. Mohr urges you to make the response piece easy to understand. "Publisher's Clearinghouse can make you hunt for all the pieces needed to return the mailing, but you shouldn't make your students do so."

24. Make sure you understand that the purpose of the Search letter is for generating leads only, says Royall. Don't use the letter to try to sell your prospects on the institution. A college education is a big-ticket item and selecting one is a multi-step process. He also suggests not including a brochure in with your letter — you don't want to give the students a reason

to turn you down; you want them to return your card.

25. Affleck adds: copyreading and proofreading are two different things and both must be done. The copy should flow. Two sets of eyes are better than one for proofing.

For more information, contact:

Arthur Affleck, State System of Higher Education, 2986 N. Second St., Harrisburg, PA 17110; Ph:717/720-4176; Joan Isaac Mohr, Quinnipiac College, Mount Carmel Ave., Hamden, CT 06518; Ph: 203/288-5251; or William Royall,10001 Patterson Ave., Suite 100, Richmond, VA 23233; Ph: 804/741-8965. (December 1994)

Ethical Technology Increases Delivery Options

When we first talked with Joe Head, director of admissions at Kennesaw State College (GA), about using telemarketing to recruit students (*Recruitment and Retention*, January 1990), he was already applying telephone technology to his next project.

Head was using automated dialing and announcing devices (ADAD) — more commonly known as computerized outbound calling — to expand his office personnel's strength at Kennesaw, a public, commuter institution with 12,000 students.

Head is quick to point out that computerized outbound calling is not a replacement for a live voice in many situations, nor should it be used as a first-line recruitment tool. "It's a support device that should be positioned later in the recruitment process as a notification system," he stresses.

His greatest success with ADAD is in its use as a status report announcement delivery system. For example, Head uses it to contact applicants who are missing documents by "matching and batching" a group of outbound calls with the same message.

The computer dials each student's number and leaves a message notifying him/her of the missing document. The system allows the student to verify receipt of the message and leave one after the computer is done.

A staff member calls up the previous evening's list to see how many numbers the computer made contact with. "We've found that generally, 30% of the messages are delivered directly to the student, 30% are delivered to someone in the student's family, and the rest are busy, no answers, or other nonresponsive calls," says Head.

He also implements ADAD when his office needs to get out a quick announcement. Four weeks before the start of the summer quarter of 1991, the University of Georgia Regents required that all new students be immunized before enrolling. A mass postcard mailing, coupled with a computerized outbound call, reminded students of this requirement.

"The sequential and diverse blitz of reminder messages quickly produced results," says Head. "And this multiple 'layered massaging system' is now typical of our office's communication style."

Student Reaction

Overall, Head says student reaction to the computerized voice has been positive. "We may get a negative response from one out of 100 calls," he says.

Head uses ADAD only with those who've applied for admission or who want to be readmitted. "In our letters and literature, we tell students that they may expect to receive a call from the college," he says, "although we don't say it may be from a computer." Students who leave a message on the automated system are thanked in a subsequent letter.

To ensure that the system was effective and not offensive, during the first year of use Head's phonathon staff called students the night after they had received a computer call. "Many responded with comments like: 'It made Kennesaw State look like it was in the 21st century' or 'The school I'm going to attend is really on the cutting-edge.' "

Concerned about the potential for misuse, Head emphasizes that institutions should use the technology only as a part of a comprehensive enrollment management plan. "Those of us who are professional enrollment officers should only engage in this in the best of taste, and practice it with the highest of ethics," he cautions. And many state legislatures agree.

In Georgia, the legislature forbids computerized outbound calls to originate within the state. But the regulations do allow nonprofit organizations who register with the state's Public Service Commission to use the technology.

Users must abide by strict regulations. "Technically, you can only contact those you've established a relationship with," cautions Head. "Those who want to use this technology in good faith must investigate their state laws."

The cost of this technology is surprisingly reasonable — systems range from $800-$2500. Colleges may incur additional costs if they don't have a 486 PC and a dedicated phone line.

For more information, contact:

Joe Head, Director of Admissions,Kennesaw State College, P.O. Box 444, Marietta, GA 30061; Ph: 404/423-6311. (May 1994)

Ed. note: Head has written a telemarketing book called *Phone Power for College Admissions and the Communications Explosion.* To order, contact: Collegiate Telemarketing Institute, P.O. Box 2363, Cartersville, GA 30120; Ph: 800/606-1015.

Recruitment with a "Flip of the Switch"

Martha Keune, admissions representative at the Calmar campus of Northeast Iowa Community College, accomplished the feat of being in two places at once with just a "flip of the switch."

The switch is connected to the new Iowa Communications Network, the statewide, state-of-the-art, fiber-optic network installed primarily for distance learning. The network connects the state's three regional universities, all of its community colleges, Iowa Public Television, and a K-12 site from each of the state's 99 counties.

While the system's original intent was to deliver course programming to remote sites, Keune saw other applications. "I just thought that, if we can have classes being offered at different high schools, why can't I recruit with it?" she says.

So she connected the campus with two area high schools and presented a one-hour session on NICC to all of their seniors — without any of them having to leave their sites.

Before the electronic visit, Keune mailed a packet of materials that included a financial aid brochure and a catalog. While on the air, Keune reviewed the material as well as answered questions.

Because the program originated from campus, the set-up allowed students to talk with representatives from NICC's financial aid office, the learning center, the counseling center, and a current NICC student.

Although it's too early to tell the impact of the visit on recruitment, Keune does say she will do it again next year — as an adjunct to, not a replacement for, a personal visit.

Despite the lack of a personal touch, using the network to recruit is cost-effective. Instead of incurring the costs of driving to both sites with the additional college staff, the network cost only $5 an hour (per site) for maintenance fees. For $15, she was able to visit two cities and reach all of their seniors at one time.

The network was partially funded with a two-year, $8 million STAR schools grant from the Dept. of Education, which picked up half the cost of installing monitors and cameras at each site, explains Kathy Guilgot, NICC's director of telecommunications. The institutions picked up the rest. The state bore the cost of putting in the fiber cable.

For more information, contact:

Martha Keune, Admissions Representative or Kathy Guilgot, Director of Telecommunications, Northeast Iowa Community College, Calmar Campus, Box 400, Calmar, IA 52132; Ph: 319/562-3263; Fax: 319/562-3719. (May 1994)

Video Brings Four-Year Campuses to Future Transfer Students

Peter Vogt, Editor, National On-Campus Report

Editor's note: This article first appeared in Recruitment and Retention's sister publication, National On-Campus Report.

Patricia Makowsky, coordinator of transfer services at Ulster County Community College (NY), figured students would tune her out if she simply lectured to them about their future at four-year campuses.

So, she got reports from the field.

Makowsky and Bob Hill, coordinator of media resources, took a video camera and microphone to four-year schools near Stone Ridge (where UCCC is located) and talked with former Ulster students about the ups and downs of transferring. The result: a videotape for Ulster students, who can watch it to get the scoop on transferring from familiar, trustworthy sources.

Makowsky says she got the idea for the video almost four years ago, when she ran into some former Ulster students who had gone through nearly opposite experiences at their new campuses.

Two biology students, who had gone on to a "rather prestigious college," had been dismissed after partying for an entire semester. Another student said the competition at her new school had been so intense that she had spent most of her time studying.

"I thought there must be a happy medium between the two clowns and the gal who felt pressure to keep up," Makowsky says. "I thought there must be something we could do as a two-year school to prepare transfer students for what's ahead of them."

So she approached Hill with her idea and got the run-down on producing a video. She and Hill then outlined the program, put questions together, tracked down former students who were willing to go on camera, and started shooting at several locations.

They wound up with about four hours' worth of footage — and sore eyes, no doubt, after hours in the editing suite.

"There was a tremendous amount of editing — more than I anticipated," Makowsky says. "I had not a clue how hard it would be.

"For example, I thought the first person I interviewed was marvelous. She had outstanding presence and was very articulate. When it came time to edit, her answer was wonderful, but didn't quite make sense because we didn't want to include the question I had asked. There were lots of technical things like that that I hadn't anticipated."

The two eventually produced a 20-minute video, starring students who discuss issues like managing time, living with roommates, making grades, social situations, avoiding distractions, making friends, and joining clubs and organizations. Makowsky says the tape has received good reviews from students, who can watch it at campus screenings or check it out overnight. The convenience makes it more accessible to the students.

"I could stand in front of them and talk but it wouldn't have much effect. ... But if they can watch former students who say,'I wish I knew then what I know now,' that's something they can really use."

For more information, contact:

Patricia Makowsky, Coordinator of Transfer Services, Ulster County Community College, Student Development Center, Stone Ridge, NY 12484; Ph: 914/687-5091. (October 1992)

Database Provides Access to Distance Learning Opportunities

Satisfying a student's request for a correspondence course can be as simple as turning on your computer, thanks to Distance Learn.

Distance Learn is a searchable database of college credit opportunities at a distance developed by Regents College (NY), the oldest and largest assessment unit in the U.S. The external degree program of the University of the State of New York, Regents helps people obtain academic recognition for what they've already learned.

The database includes over 7,000 courses and exams. None have site-based requirements for credit and all are from regionally accredited institutions or approved testing agencies.

Distance Learn includes information on how to obtain the course work, how courses fit into overall academic programs, descriptions and costs, and length of time for program completion. Distance Learn also includes a section on external graduate programs.

Donn Aiken, assistant director of The Institute for Distance Learning, says the database helps Regents College "try to play the brokering role the college has always played in education."

Regents offers only proficiency exams, not courses. Academic advisors evaluate students' educational documents and help them plan how to finish their degrees using exams and courses in their communities and at a distance. Since many of the advisors' case loads averaged 500 students, Aiken says, "they needed something that would help them sort through all of the offerings."

The program runs on any personal computer with MS-DOS and a hard disk with 3 MB available. It requires no special knowledge to install or operate and uses a simple menu system with on-screen help.

Regents College will license Distance Learn to other schools for an annual fee of $99. The fee includes a user manual, computer disks, and a free update in six months.

Aiken stresses that the college isn't trying to make a fortune with the program. "It's more important to help students reach their goals than to make money," he says.

For more information, contact:

Donn Aiken, Assistant Director, Institute for Distance Learning, Regents College, 7 Columbia Circle, Albany, NY 12203; Ph: 518/464-8765. (July 1993)

PRIZM Helps Refine Search

Many schools are increasing the number of students they mail to just to hold enrollments steady, but David Murray, director of admissions at DePauw University (IN), is taking the road less traveled. Thanks to PRIZM, a licensed market segmentation system, Murray substantially trimmed the number of Search names he mails to, yet keeps his entering class stable.

Demographers have long known that people tend to live, or cluster, in areas that reflect their social and economic values. PRIZM — a lifestyle segmentation product of the Claritas Corporation — applies a mathematical clustering technique to census data. Each of the 62 resulting cluster types is homogeneous and distinct from the others.

Claritas officials named the clusters to describe the types of residents of particular areas. For instance, "Blue Blood Estates" describes the wealthiest neighborhoods. "Shotguns and Pickups," "Kids and Cul-de-sacs," and "Bohemian Mix" represent other populations.

"The principle behind PRIZM is 'birds of a feather flock together,'" explains Tim Dodge, senior vice president of College Marketing Technologies (CAT), a company that adapts PRIZM system for higher education. "We can ascribe a tremendous number of geodemographic details simply using an address," he points out. "The technology is so sophisticated, one can target individual household levels."

Consumer products companies use PRIZM to find new customers or to launch a product. Some admissions officers, like Murray, use it to improve prospecting and reduce printing and mailing costs.

Finding More Students
Like Your Current Students

"The expectation is that you need more numbers to get more inquiries, which will result in more applications to get the required number of matriculants," says Dodge. "But many schools, in the fervor to get numbers, don't pay as much attention to matching the students with the institution."

PRIZM helps make that match by building a profile of the student body which has historically matriculated at a particular institution. After constructing the profile, "we can stamp it on the primary draw area and show them specifically in which areas they need to trim or invest more time," adds Dodge. That is, PRIZM can tell what current students are like and where to find more of them.

A DePauw graduate who's a vice president for General Foods convinced Murray to try PRIZM. "He invited me to a training session where I heard about it," he explains. "After seeing what it was doing for Kodak and IBM, I decided to see what it could do for us."

So Murray took his entire student body — two years' worth of data on applicants, admits, and enrolled — and had it analyzed according to cluster types. The first year, he sent his Search names through the PRIZM methodology and prioritized them for mailing.

He discovered that the highest priority group — as indicated by PRIZM — turned out to have the highest application rate — 10%. The lowest priority group also applied low — 2%.

After using PRIZM the second year, he trimmed names he felt wouldn't pay off. "We bought more Search names knowing we were going to throw some away," Murray explains. Dodge adds that some admissions officers, reluctant to eliminate names, will send a less expensive publication or send publications bulk rate.

Murray also uses PRIZM to help target special messages to specific groups, particularly middle-income students. "The only way you can have a shot at those who are middle-income," he explains, "is to intercept them at an early juncture."

He notes, "Those who are middle-income know they won't get aid, so they rule out applying based on cost. We want to reach them with the message that this is one college that looks at that issue."

With PRIZM, Murray has found he can isolate an income range on tax returns. He's discovered one cluster type whose families are considered middle-income that generates over 70% of DePauw's financial aid applications. "When we mail to similar families," he explains, "we can now go to them with a middle-income message."

While Murray uses PRIZM to help him convince middle-income students of DePauw's affordability, other schools hope that PRIZM can help them improve diversity on their campuses.

Financial problems may cause still others to search for more no-need students. Dodge warns against this practice: "If schools with lots of high-need students try to turn that around by recruiting lots of low-need ones, they're going to find that Blue Blood types don't fit in on their campus and, if they come, don't stay. So retention suffers."

Dodge admits PRIZM won't work well for schools that recruit locally or don't use direct mail or advertising. Clients who expect PRIZM to triple their response rates will be disappointed, as will those who misinterpret or do a less than satisfactory execution of the analysis. "A lift factor of 20%-30% is reasonable to expect," says Dodge.

The cost will make an admissions director take a hard look at the budget, but Dodge says that PRIZM saves money in the long run. "Most clients can reduce publication and mailing costs by 17%-30%," he notes.

The basic profile and analysis, including maps, charts, and zip codes broken down state by state, runs $10,750. Prioritizing mailing lists will cost a client $2850 per list plus $30 for each 1,000 records. CAT also compiles a database of student names and can supply school-matched names as early as the sophomore year.

While PRIZM and similar systems may be the newest tool for finding students, Murray offers a word of caution: "It [PRIZM] must be used carefully. Admissions directors must use it with some intuition and experience behind it." Dodge echoes the admonition: "Like a chain saw, PRIZM is a powerful tool. In the wrong hands, it's dangerous. But in the right hands, it's a fantastic technology."

For more information, contact:

David Murray, Assistant Vice President and Director of Admissions, DePauw University, Greencastle, IN 46135; Ph: 317/658-4006; Tim Dodge, Senior Vice President, College Marketing Technologies, 22 Crystal Lake Plaza, Crystal Lake, IL 60014-7929; Ph: 815/455-1951. (July 1991)

College Encourages "Test Drive" of Academic Computer

To familiarize prospective students with the quality of academic computing on its campus, The College of Wooster (OH) lets accepted applicants "test drive" the equipment before deciding to enroll.

The college uses its system as a means of helping students distinguish Wooster from similar institutions. The system also underscores the college's commitment to computing beyond the computer science major. "It's simply a way of demonstrating a first-rate computer center in the same way others would demonstrate a world-class library on a campus tour," says Hayden Schilling, dean of admissions.

"We've been recognized as one of the leaders of undergraduate academic computing," he adds. The system emphasizes "the availability of resources we have to offer — among them, computing."

Applicants also benefit. Students, who may view the computer only as a word processor, can see the various capabilities of a high-quality machine by dialing up through a modem at their convenience from home or high school. "We want to give admitted students ways of exploring Wooster prior to paying the fee," says Philip Harriman, director of academic computing.

Administering the program is both simple and inexpensive. "Any college with dial-in lines to its computer system can implement a similar program," says Harriman. Accepted applicants receive letters containing user names and passwords that allow them to enter Wooster's VAX computer — normally used for statistical purposes and electronic mail. A large fiber-optic network links the computers to the residence halls and all of the academic buildings.

The 1600 students Wooster admits each year cause little interference for other users. Rather than setting up a name and a password for each, Harriman reserves 100 names and passwords, then assigns them to groups of 17 to 20 students. He says his office hasn't received any complaints about sharing names and passwords.

Wooster's admissions schedule also reduces interference. Since the college doesn't have rolling admissions, early-decision students are admitted in December, with the remaining applicants receiving notices in March and April. "By the time the largest group is admitted," notes Harriman, "it's the end of the academic year."

In five years Harriman has seen no abuses of the privilege. "We're talking to a liberal arts group of students," he explains. "And although we've had students from as far away as New Jersey and Arizona log-in, few of them actually use the system. Those that do, don't use much other than the bulletin boards." And most students experiment with the system as "a result of parental interest."

For more information, contact:

Hayden Schilling, Dean of Admissions, or Philip Harriman, Director of Academic Computing, College of Wooster, Wooster, OH 44691; Ph: 216/263-2118 (Schilling) or 263-2283 (Harriman). (March 1991)

Effective Telemarketing Boosts Commuter College's Growth

Kennesaw State College, one of five schools within a 35-mile radius of Atlanta, attracts a lot of interest from "college shoppers" — prospective students who often choose "the best deal." Kennesaw has turned this potential disadvantage into an advantage: it uses telemarketing to turn "shoppers" into "buyers." As a result it's one of the fastest-growing colleges in Georgia — doubling its enrollment in just eight years.

Kennesaw's success story stems from emphasizing the telephone in its marketing strategy. With the communication explosion affecting all businesses, Joe Head, director of admissions, feels that educators who use telemarketing are "closer to the forefront."

"We can incorporate already installed technology as one of the more effective tools in our arsenal," says Head. "We have the capabilities to stop and study the results, to shape behavior on the phone, and to use the medium with dignity and integrity. With a carefully shaped strategy, anyone's reachable."

But even the best marketing in the world isn't effective unless the product is good. And Kennesaw is ambitious about improving its quality. "Kennesaw is like a penny stock with a lot of equity," says Head. "Our degree is appreciating like real estate. We're adding programs, professors receive requests for consulting, and enrollment is climbing."

Telemarketing strategy involves inbound calls as well as outbound. "You're not seeing the big picture if you just consider outbound calls," notes Head. "Every time you answer the phone, the potential is there to influence the caller's behavior and eventually the college choice."

He adds, "Because the support staff is very often the first and sometimes the only contact with the institution students have before they enroll, support staff can be a very heavy player in the recruitment game."

Because of the composition of Kennesaw's student body — the average age is 27 — Head emphasizes telemarketing with three specific groups: incompletes, readmits, and specialty groups. "Many of those students are adults," notes Head. "They respond more readily to a phone call than they do to direct mail."

The Attitude Is Service, Not Sales/Marketing

To convert the incompletes, Head ran a student phonathon to notify pending applicants of their status and to get a more accurate count of those who would actually follow through and enroll. "We made courtesy calls about two weeks before the deadline of the quarter to new, incoming students," says Head. "These calls were made with a service attitude, not a sales/marketing one."

Students who stop-out stay active in the registrar's office for four quarters, then become inactive. Head saw potential in the inactive population and held a student phonathon to contact people who had attended five to 10 quarters earlier and were eligible to return.

"The phonathon ran for four evenings," says Head. "We started with between 1000 and 1500 eligible readmits. The students completed about 300 calls." And the results were rewarding: of the completed calls, about 20% reactivated and 60% of those eventually enrolled.

"In three years we've nearly doubled the readmit enrollment rate. And while students may not activate for the target quarter, there's a residual bonus if they activate for a later term as a result of the call."

Head uses student groups for the phonathons, "multiple groups to avoid burnout," he notes. "They're either paid hourly or we make a donation to the group's treasury. We also let them make a long-distance call at the end of the evening as a perk." He added that "Sunday school or senior citizen groups — if properly trained — could be as effective."

Because of the volume of calls, using staff would be a burden. "They would view it as a penalty or punishment," observes Head. "However, I give the staff the opportunity to be involved by turning the phonathons into a management operation." One staff member now coordinates all telemarketing.

Telemarketing can also be used to reach precisely selected targets, such as minority groups or honors students. Head recently finished contacting 62 alumni children who are in the process of choosing a college. "A personal phone call from the director of admissions was certainly more impressive than another letter with my signature," says Head. "I was able to gauge their level of interest and target follow-up materials more effectively. And because I've color-coded the applications, I'll eventually know how productive these calls were."

Head offered the telephone as a response to the commuter environment. As a result, success is just a ring away.

For more information, contact:

Joe F. Head, Director of Admissions, Kennesaw State College, Marietta, GA 30061; Ph: 404/423-6311. (January 1990)

A resource for telemarketing is *Phone Power for College Admissions,* which includes cassette tapes for counselors and support staff, a handbook on conducting phonathons and a notebook for staff training.

To order, contact:

The Collegiate Telemarketing Institute, P.O. Box 2363, Cartersville, GA 30120; Ph: 800/606-1015.

Creative Computer Technology Invades Admissions Office

The entry of computers into the admissions office has reduced paperwork, shortened turnaround time for processing, and improved tracking of applications. While most institutions use the computer for these purposes, others devise imaginative uses with an eye toward the 21st century. The University of Richmond and University of Wisconsin System, for example, have developed interesting ways to improve application processing and information delivery.

University of Richmond CAP

In an effort to relieve the ever-increasing paper jam, the University of Richmond's admissions office asked its in-house computer staff to transfer its paper application form onto a floppy disk compatible with both IBM and Apple computers and reproduce it in quantity. "It's not the latest in a series of gimmicks," stresses Thomas Pollard, Jr., dean of admissions. "It's a way of making our office more efficient and serving our students better."

Students learned about the computerized application on the inquiry card of the search mailing. Those who requested the disk received an application package which included special instructions and a code sheet to help boot up and run it. To ensure that all of the data is accurate and honest, students must sign a form stating such.

When returned, the completed disks are downloaded into the mainframe and turned into paper. A major benefit of this process is the accuracy. Says Pollard, "Our data processing people love it. If a student's name has an unusual spelling, it will *always* be spelled that way. It's the most accurate system that I know of."

Before duplicating thousands of disks, Pollard enlisted several hundred Advanced Placement computer science students to check for bugs. He mailed the disk with an application packet and encouraged them to try it out. Pollard discovered that students couldn't return to a previous screen — they had to go back to the beginning and run the program again. "Needless to say, we corrected that problem before sending any out," says Pollard.

Last year's mailing of over 500 disks resulted in 100 completed applications, which led to 35 eventual enrollments. And only one of the 35 indicated an intent to major in computer science. "Students indicated pre-med as their number one choice of major, with business running a strong second," says Pollard. "And what's even more interesting is the majority of students who used the disk or indicated they'd use it have worked with computers since fifth grade."

While the disk has proved beneficial to admissions, it also provided information to the housing office. UR officials discovered they'll need to rewire all the dorm rooms as well as reconfigure the furniture to create space for students who want to bring their PCs to campus.

Although student reactions to the disk are positive, Pollard notes many of those who submitted a computerized application also filled out the paper one. "It's like corn flakes in a jar," he says. "A jar keeps corn flakes fresh and prevents them from crumbling. But there's a cultural bias against corn flakes in anything other than a box."

While disks increase the cost of the application by $2 to $3, the ease of processing justifies the increase. Pollard estimates each application package — a prospectus-type booklet, paper application, disk, return cardboard mailer, and application activator to collect the fee — runs between $6.50 and $7.00 to produce and mail.

Pollard is sold on the computerized application: "It's the wave of the future." He adds, "To encourage more prospective students to submit their application on disk, we are considering a reduction of the application fee."

1995 Update:

The Computerized Application Process program was discontinued at Richmond. Bill Mallon from the Admissions Office sent us the following update in order to assist others planning or carrying out similar programs.

The Demise of the CAP

The Computerized Application Process (CAP) never produced the results that were intended when it was developed in 1988. The CAP was produced to save time on both ends: it would be easier for the technologically advanced student to complete, and it would save data entry time for the admissions office.

The first goal was most likely achieved. The second, however, was not. The completed disks never were able to be downloaded into our mainframe. (Tom Pollard was overly optimistic when first interviewed for this article.) In fact, it actually forced more handling time per application than did a paper application: the CAP had to be inserted into a PC, printed out on paper, and then entered into the computer system as all paper applications.

When the program was first produced in 1988, it was a first — and like many "firsts" it was well-received. Since that time, however, technology has advanced at a staggering pace and, as the years passed, the CAP looked way behind the time. Students who were used to high-tech video games with graphics as good as real life were not impressed with CAP's unsophisticated presentation.

The program never proved cost-effective, either. When the program first came out in the late 1980's, the returns were good. After the novelty of the CAP wore off, its advantage declined. For instance:

	Fall 1988*	Fall 1990	Fall 1993
CAPs sent out	153	1081	1000
Applications received	57	68	51
Acceptance	30	44	33
Enrolled	18	21	7

*Test group of students with interest in computer science.

In the beginning, a majority of students using the CAP who were admitted decided to enroll (60% in 1988, 48% in 1990). However, by 1993, only 21% of those CAP students who were admitted decided to enroll. The CAP was a good recruiting tool when it was new, but its influence declined as other colleges and outside vendors developed similar programs.

It is also obvious that students still prefer the paper application. The return (percentage of applications received of those sent out) was never that good — in 1993, only 5%.

Finally, other reasons to abandon our own CAP is that the Common Application, which we accept, developed its own computer application this year. It's distributed free to interested students and doesn't cost us anything beyond our normal participation fee in Common Application. It also performs much better than our own did. I believe the Common Application was developed by Peterson's.

University of Wisconsin System Provides Transfer Assistance

Students seeking to transfer often lack information they need to make appropriate transfer decisions. A program, developed jointly by the University of Wisconsin System administration and the 14 System institutions, is designed to fill this information gap and alleviate some of the hassles of transferring.

The Transfer Information System (TIS) is a computerized information program accessed over the Internet for UW System and the Wisconsin Technical College System (WTCS) institutions. Funding for they system came from the Wisconsin legislature, says Gail Bergman, TIS project coordinator, to serve both UW institutions and the technical colleges.

The goal is to give transfer students easy access to complete information, enabling them to make sound transfer decisions. It also will provide admissions staffs across the state with an effective system to communicate course and program changes.

Work on TIS began in March 1988. TIS is now up and running at all UW schools and at five Wisconsin Technical College campuses accross the state. It enables students to plan in advance, knowing how courses taken at one institution will transfer to another institution.

When fully implemented, it also will provide information about how the courses they take will apply toward the requirements of a particular degree program.

Bergman and her colleagues made sure that TIS was user-friendly. Students, faculty, and staff need no previous knowledge of computers to operate the system. Response to the system has been positive. Students, in particular, appreciate having current and accurate transfer information at their fingertips.

For more information, contact

Larry Rubin, TIS Project Administrator, UW System Administration, 1610 Van Hise Hall, 1220 Linden Dr., Madison, WI 53706; Phone: 608/262-6717; Gail Bergman, TIS Project Coordinator, 1646 Van Hise Hall, 1220 Linden Drive, Madison, WI 53706; Phone: 608/262-6718; or Bill Mallon, Admissions Office, University of Richmond, Richmond, VA 23173; Phone: 804/289-8640. (May 1990)

TQM Changes Admissions from Impossible to Accomplished

Pressured by dwindling enrollments and tightened finances, a growing number of schools are adopting the philosophy of total quality management (TQM).

TQM focuses on achieving quality through continuous improvement. Its key tenets involve empowering workers, staying close to customers, and assuming workers want to do a good job.

Oregon State University, in 1990, organized its first team in the physical plant. After seeing significant results, it wasn't long before decision-makers focused their attention on the admissions office. John Byrne, president of OSU, deciding TQM could help improve the admissions process, created teams to look at five areas: application evaluations, the flow of mail, graduate admissions, recruitment, and retention. Bruce Shepard, Director of Undergraduate Programs, headed the application evaluation team, composed of all the evaluators and head advisors and nicknamed "Admissions Impossible."

The team, it turned out, was aptly named. "We made a flowchart of the evaluation process and it looked like spaghetti and meatballs," says Shepard. "We found that 95% of the problems were with the process and not with people."

After surveying their "customers" — applicants, high school and community college counselors, alumni, and head OSU advisors — the team conducted phone interviews with selected members of each group.

"Our goal was to reduce the amount of time it took to make an admissions decision," says Shepard.

Admissions Accomplished

Shepard and his team eventually reduced the number of days for an admissions decision from 67 to 6.7 days. He admits that the reduction came with a substantial change.

"We had to change the evaluators' attitude from that of a gatekeeper — preventing the university from getting a poor student — to serving those who applied," says Shepard.

Changing the culture also meant changing the evaluators' reliance on rules, formulas, and procedures to a reliance on their judgment.

OSU's use of SAT scores was another area ripe for improvement. While the system requires all students to submit SAT scores, OSU uses them only in borderline cases — when the student's work isn't good enough for admittance, says Shepard. "Unfortunately, we were holding up even the decisions of 4.0 applicants because they hadn't sent in their scores." They made the decision to admit future applicants whose grades made them obvious acceptances without scores.

TQM also helped the team reduce the number of cases sent to the admissions committee. "We did this by letting faculty get to know the evaluators, to develop faith and trust in them and their judgment," Shepard explains.

From Skeptic to Believer

As with any major cultural change, team members had a great deal of skepticism about TQM. Even though Byrne had promised not to eliminate positions, evaluators knew that the results of previous teams had led to some reassignments. "When the president appointed five teams to look into admissions, they felt the heat on the back of their necks," admits Shepard.

"Benchmarking" — measuring an institution's processes, procedures, products, and performance against other similar institutions — helped spur some of the changes. "Benchmarking helped those people who had been with OSU for 20 years and thought that the way OSU did things was the only way to do it," explains Shepard.

Shepard stresses that evaluators had seen the need for a number of the changes over the years but didn't have hope that the changes would occur. Afterwards, they wouldn't let the changes stop. They'd question the progress of items brought up six months earlier.

Shepard cautions that TQM is no quick fix. "It took the team about 1½ years from start to finish. We held meetings every week or one every two weeks during our crunch period."

Was it worth it? Shepard thinks the team's new name says it all — "Admissions Accomplished."

For more information, contact:

Bruce Shepard, Director, Undergraduate Academic Programs, Office of Academic Affairs, Oregon State University, Corvallis, OR 97331; Ph: 503/737-0737. (September 1991)

Contract Provides Second Chance

An unusual contract is the cornerstone of a very successful transfer program at George Mason University (VA).

The contract gives a second chance to Virginia students who've been denied admission directly out of high school, says George Gangloff, associate dean of admissions.

"As admissions has become more competitive for freshmen," he says, "we developed a program for those students who we had a strong desire to accommodate but were unable to because of their high school records."

Since 1985, GMU has interviewed students who respond to its rejection letter and who made Mason their first choice. During the interview, the admissions officer writes a contract guaranteeing admission to GMU if the student takes specific courses and earns a 2.5 GPA or associate degree at his/her local community college.

"The contract insists that the student complete one year at the community college," says Gangloff. "If a student wants to spend two years there, we've outlined programs of study for the associate degree. It's the student's choice."

Gangloff explains the contract's origin: "As the popularity of GMU increased and the applicant pool grew, we recognized that we were being forced to deny entrance to students — because of space constraints — who we knew could do well. We wanted to offer an alternative."

GMU's primary feeder institution is the 35,000-student Northern Virginia Community College (NOVA) with its five campuses, all within 10-15 miles of Mason. However, Gangloff points out that GMU "would do a contract with any college."

Although GMU admits a substantial number of transfers each year, Gangloff says, "we've never tracked the number of contracts we've written. The number [of students] that come and talk to us after being denied is about 100 a year. But thousands go to the community colleges and say they want to go to Mason."

Widespread Knowledge Means Students Self-Select

Since 1983, GMU has published recommended courses of study and course requirements for all of its 50 majors and distributed them to each community college.

"Because we've published information on our requirements for years, students who don't meet the requirements know that they won't get in," Gangloff says. This explains the limited numbers who take advantage of the contract. Gangloff notes that GMU has usually admitted at least as many transfers as first-year students. Last year, it enrolled 3,000 transfers, compared with 1,750 students without college experience.

Of those 3,000 transfers, 65% had taken courses at community colleges and transferred nearly 100,000 courses to GMU. "Our kids use the community colleges to the max," Gangloff remarks. On average, one out of four students who transfer from Virginia's community colleges enrolls at GMU — with two out of three of those coming from NOVA.

Suggestions for Establishing Similar Programs

Gangloff's advice to those who want to set up a similar program is to first sell the idea to the faculty.

"I knew that the response I would get when I first broached the subject [of serving transfers] was: 'We don't want any more of those kind.' But I also knew that faculty respect research. So I pulled out the studies to convince them that 'those kind' were successful."

One of the studies showed that the average GPAs of transfer students who were ready to graduate were within one-tenth of a point of those of GMU first-year students. "The transfer students were good risks," says Gangloff.

Other advice:

Set the stage at your institution for transfers.

"It's unfair to community college transfers to bring them in in the middle of their academic career and expect them to fit in the mold developed for those students who started as freshmen," says Gangloff. "You must provide academic options."

Look at your transfer policies.

While most schools accept only transfer courses similar in content to their own, Gangloff argues that it's a conservative policy: "Our faculty were willing to accept courses not exactly identical to ours so long as they are consistent in quality."

Beat down myths that transfer students are inferior.

"Look at the performance of those transfers you've already admitted," he advises.

Be an advocate. Put yourself in the shoes of the community college counselor.

"The arrangement with the community colleges is a partner-ship," Gangloff says. "I ask myself, if I'm sitting there, what kind of information would be useful to have?" he explains.

Understanding the counselor's role led GMU to develop materials that "go right to the nitty-gritty" — for example, a table-driven, transfer credit evaluation system with information on more than 40 institutions.

"Any institution where we regularly get 15 or more students is included in the system," says Gangloff. "We print a hard copy of this information and give it to the community college counselors."

Constantly examine the process.

"This type of arrangement requires constant attention and tweaking," says Gangloff. The Inter-Institutional Articulation Committee — composed of senior administrators, counselors, and faculty from GMU and NOVA — meets regularly throughout the year. The committee oversees issues handled by representatives from specific disciplines.

GMU's attitude contributes to the program's success. "Work-ing with the community colleges ... is, to quote the Quaker Oatmeal commercial, 'the right thing to do,' " Gangloff says lightheartedly.

In a more serious tone, he adds:

"There was a recognition back in the '80s that the demand for public educational services in the region would outstrip GMU's and the community colleges' ability to deliver. This recognition followed a master agreement between the faculties of GMU and the community colleges in the 1970s.

"We realized that, no matter how much money we would receive from the state, it would never be enough. So we decided to maximize our resources and depend upon the community colleges to be the provider of freshman and sophomore courses."

GMU's next issue will be to develop methods for students to cross-enroll at the community colleges.

"Now we sort of expect them to finish at the community college and then come to Mason," says Gangloff. "But many students, when things got tough financially, drop to part-time and find that going to a community college is cheaper and/or more convenient.

GMU and NOVA are now cooperatively opening two new campuses of the distributed University. NOVA will offer lower-division courses on these campuses, while GMU will offer junior, senior, and graduate-level study. Consequently, the two institutions are exploring concurrent enrollment possibilities.

For more information, contact:

George Gangloff, Associate Dean of Admissions for Transfer Concerns, Office of Admissions, George Mason University, Fairfax, VA 22030-4444; Ph: 703/993-2395. (July 1993)

Retention
Strategies

Section Three

Retain Adults by Addressing their Feelings of Impostorship

Ever been in a situation where you fear being discovered as a fake? The feeling of impostorship not only emerges in social situations; research shows it's common among adult learners — even those with successful past educational experiences.

Impostors feel that, as soon as they make a slip and reveal their inadequacies, they'll be asked to leave under a cloud of shame, says Stephen Brookfield, distinguished professor in the graduate school of education at the University of St. Thomas (MN). In researching his book, *The Skillful Teacher*, he says he was struck by the number of adult students — and their teachers — who spoke about feelings of impostorship.

"I expected to uncover those feelings in students whose educational experiences had been humiliating," says Brookfield. "But I had not expected impostorship to be expressed so frequently by adults who, to my eyes, appeared confident and successful."

Brookfield conducted his research by asking adult students what it felt like to be a student. "I asked them to recount the memorable and critical events in their lives as learners — the transformative events — both the high and low points," he says. He also examined learning journals and responses to a critical incident instrument — which paints a biographical report of the student as a learner.

Brookfield discovered that feelings of impostorship came up in a number of different guises, particularly in the early stages of learning. He admits the feeling fades over time — if students are allowed to talk about it — but never disappears. Impostorship feelings also seemed to cross gender lines: both men and women said they experienced such feelings.

Brookfield speculates that students feel a sense of impostorship most when they don't know the rules of the game. "My private theory," he says, "is that those who move out of education and live in the world of work and then move back into education ... feel a heightened sense of impostorship than do those who have gone to school continuously."

Impostorship Triggers

One of the most frequently mentioned triggers to impostorship feelings was the news that the student had been accepted into an educational program. "When they find out they're accepted, they think, 'It was a bureaucratic mistake, the secretary misfiled my credentials, sooner or later I'll be asked to leave,' " Brookfield explains.

Another trigger usually occurs during the first class, when teachers have students introduce themselves in the belief that the exercise eases anxiety. "Instead of easing anxiety, it actually has an opposite effect," Brookfield says. "Many of the students are feeling that all the rest of their classmates 'seem to have done a great deal more than I have.' "

Brookfield says faculty also don't realize how tough it is for others to be critical of a printed work. Asking students to put their voices in an assignment or demonstrating their own way to perform a skill can trigger major feelings of impostorship. "Taking a critical stance is actually perceived as impertinence," he says. "Students' self-talk is usually 'What right do I have to challenge an expert?' "

What contributes to these kinds of feelings? Brookfield theorizes that "a culture that socializes us into the idea of always being in command" is responsible. "Maturity is being equated with perfect control over everything in your life," he says. "What you get promoted for is portraying a calm paragon of pedagogic virtue — not by saying that 'I'm always falling flat on my face.' "

Diminishing the Feelings

To combat feelings of impostorship, Brookfield recommends it be brought out from under the table, named, and addressed publicly. When students hear it identified, he explains, they tend to relax.

During orientation or the first few classes, upperclass students can visit the new students and talk about their experiences. "The returning students say, 'When I was in your shoes, I just felt that I would never make it through,' " says Brookfield. Teachers can also address impostorship in class by drawing on and openly expressing their own memories of learning things for the first time.

Brookfield also suggests that faculty try, as much as possible, to develop peer learning groups or assign group projects. "Any way that I can get students to cluster into small groups I do," he says.

Why are peer groups so important? Brookfield found that the single most important indicator for retaining adult students was whether the student felt like a member of a peer learning group. "Membership (in the peer learning group) was the thing people said helped them survive being an adult student," he says.

For more information, contact:

Stephen Brookfield, Distinguished Professor, Graduate School of Education, Mail #5017, University of St. Thomas, 2115 Summit Ave., St. Paul, MN 55105; Ph: 612/647-5393. (September 1992)

To order The Skillful Teacher:

Contact: Jossey-Bass Publishers, 350 Sansome St., San Francisco, CA 94104-9825; Ph: 415/433-1767. Cost: $23.95 plus $3 shipping and handling.

Orientation Program Is "For Adults Only"

by Jennifer Lind

Last fall, non-traditional students at Marywood College (PA) found some common ground, courtesy of "For Adults Only," a new orientation program for students who are older than average.

For five weeks, new students 23 and older attended seminars on study skills, support services, social networking, and campus layout. According to Jane Baker, assistant director of student development services, the seminars are designed to "meet the special needs of adult students," who make up a large percentage of Marywood's student population.

Baker and Jean Leonard, assistant dean of student development services, began the FAO program last fall. They asked the admissions office for the names of all new students 23 and older, and then sent them letters, brochures, and registration forms.

About 40 students signed up for the initial program and attended weekly seminars covering the "nuts and bolts" of returning to school, using the library, meeting other adult learners, and other pertinent topics. The program's success led to an extension of the original five-week plan to an on-going semester seminar/

self-help group. The programming of new topics evolved from discussions with students.

Many adults, Baker says, "do well in class because they're usually more serious about their education." But they need help once in a while. FAO seminars are taught by three volunteers from the counseling service. Baker says written evaluations for the first programs testify to the participants' satisfaction. "The seminars were a simple way for them to share their common concerns and needs."

For more information, contact:

Jane Baker, Assistant Director, or Sr. Jean Leonard, Assistant Dean, Student Development Services, Counseling Center, Marywood College, Scranton, PA 18509; Ph: 717/348-6245. (August 1993)

Community College Builds "Bridge" for Minority Adults

Community colleges serve over 50% of the ethnic minority students enrolled in higher education. But transfer and eventual degree completion rates remain distressingly low. Efforts to better serve these students are becoming increasingly collaborative, focusing on the critical transition between institutions. One model effort: the Tacoma Community College-Evergreen State College "Bridge Program."

Bridge offers an integrated studies curriculum to prepare students to transfer from Tacoma Community College (TCC) — primarily to Evergreen State. It provides the first two years of college work for predominantly minority, working adults. "Bridge evolved because Evergreen's administration felt they weren't effectively serving a cohort of students who really needed to be served," says Frank Garratt, then TCC vice president of academic and student affairs.

"Evergreen was getting students who wanted to go to its Tacoma campus but who didn't have the course prerequisites," he says. "Because the Tacoma campus is located in TCC's district and only offers upper-division courses, Evergreen couldn't provide the lower-division classes the students needed."

The key to Bridge is the curriculum — a team-taught, learning community model, involving faculty members from both institutions. Patterned after Evergreen's unique curriculum at its main campus in Olympia, all classes are interdisciplinary. Garratt notes that the faculty "don't know exactly what they'll teach until they plan it out."

Students enjoy the interconnectedness of the classes. "As adults, they've experienced life," says Garratt. "They're aware of the artificiality of dividing knowledge up into tidy packages. ... The learning community atmosphere encourages students to work together," he adds. "They don't see themselves in competition with each other and they help each other learn."

On the other hand, that interdisciplinary aspect requires administrative flexibility not found in most institutions. The traditional undergraduate program prepares students for transfer by requiring them to complete a certain number of courses in specific areas. But Bridge's interdisciplinary nature and team-taught efforts don't always allow TCC to package the classes tidily according to the catalog. And Garratt admits that Bridge may be of little help to students who want to attend any other four-year school than Evergreen.

Bridge's administrative structure is as collaborative as its curriculum: administrators from both campuses run the program. TCC provides most of the student services — admissions, financial aid, records — on Evergreen's campus. Bridge students pay TCC's tuition until they enroll in the upper-division courses.

Bridge understands "these students have 'life' distractions — children, jobs." The program makes allowances for these distractions and works *with* the students. Garratt says, "We tell them that we have something which we feel is of value to them and we'll help them take advantage of it the best that they can."

The learning community emphasis contributes to the program's success. Faculty recognize that students have great potential and a lot to contribute. "It's not a place where students have to prove themselves in order to be respected," says Garratt. "A lot of these students have had very negative experiences with education. This program is seen by many as a place where they can succeed."

And succeed they do. Over the past five years, Bridge has retained over 90% of its students. The campus climate contributes to the huge success. Garratt notes that Bridge "aims to reinforce or establish a sense of self-esteem among the students, related to the expectations that they can do the work and contribute to the program."

Despite the curriculum's constant restructuring, Garratt is pleased to be a part of its administration. "There's more uncertainty that rides with the program than most administrators would feel comfortable with. But, overall, it's worth it."

For more information, contact:

Katherine Hiyane-Brown, Vice President, Academic and Student Affairs, Tacoma Community College, 5900 S. 12th St., Tacoma, WA 98465; Ph: 206/566-5022. (October 1990)

Advisors Beat the Budget-Cut Blues

Lately, few institutions find themselves immune from the effects of tight budgets. As resources fail to keep pace with demand, student services — particularly advising — are asked to make do with less.

But all is not gloomy. Boston University and the University of Toledo (OH) offer some creative solutions to help ease the impact of cuts on advising programs.

Think Creatively about External Funding

"At Boston University, everything is done on a cost-effective basis," says Thomas Kerr, associate dean of engineering. "Part of what you have to do (to get additional funds) is be creative."

That attitude has enabled Kerr to increase — rather than eliminate — the number of advising programs for the College of Engineering over the past several years. His secret: external sources of funding.

Kerr explains his approach. "You don't go out and look for a grant that funds advising. What you look for are grants that want to improve, say, the retention rate of special populations. Then, you look for opportunities to fold academic advising into them."

Kerr illustrates his advice with several successes. In 1991, BU received three National Science Foundation grants to develop undergraduate research opportunities. BU based the proposals on its Freshman Research Opportunity Program. Through FROP, 25 non-matriculated students came to campus for five weeks to work with faculty on research projects.

Under the NSF grants, 30 undergraduates — from BU and other institutions — worked with faculty on research during a 10-week summer session. (The program was so popular, Kerr had to choose the 17 non-BU students from a pool of 805 applicants.)

Kerr says, "While the grants don't directly have to do with academic advising, they're a great retention tool."

BU submitted a National Institutes of Health grant proposal to fund programs for minority students enrolled in health professions at senior colleges.

As part of the proposal, Kerr contacted three local community colleges with high minority enrollments and developed a joint project. "With the grant," he says, "we will not only do on-site tutoring but we're also developing a computerized academic advising program and computerized tutorials. There will be a system at each of the community colleges as well as one at BU."

Also folded into the NIH grant was money for academic support, including funds for additional staff, outreach programming to high schools, faculty development, and peer tutoring.

Kerr points out that federal grants aren't the only source of external funding. Corporations also represent a significant resource. At BU, United Technologies funded a student lounge and offices for all student engineering organizations, as well as a Macintosh computer and a printer for student use.

Even foreign countries can be a source of extra funds for advising. Several years ago, BU developed a 3-2 engineering program with a school in Greece. "In agreement for us helping them develop their courses and texts," says Kerr, "they provide an academic counselor at BU to help advise the 3-2 students. But, the balance of that counselor's time goes to help other students."

Kerr offers these tips for successful proposal writing:

- **Schedule** — Begin with the final date the proposal needs to be postmarked. Plan backward to establish all preceding dates.

- **Preamble** — Set the proper context for the reviewers. Essential facts about the institution's mission, size, history, or other descriptors are important.

- **Introduction** — Make the strongest case about the importance of the project here. Show that the school has the capacity to conduct the proposed project by describing previous projects.

- **Program Objectives** — Provide the reviewers with quantifiable and measurable objectives and intended outcomes that will convince them this program will make a difference.

- **Strategy for Implementation** — Detail the activities and their schedule. List major phases of the operation to make it clear to the reviewers when you'll achieve your objectives.

- **Organizational Structure** — Identify program participants, their qualifications, roles, and responsibilities, and how their qualifications relate to meeting objectives.

- **Facilities** — Identify what unique equipment, laboratories, and facilities will be used to achieve the program's objectives.

- **Evaluation** — Plan and describe the evaluation findings as though they will be used to support another proposal for funds to follow up work of the current program.

- **Budget** — Demonstrate that the budget is reasonable for the objectives and scope of the project. All costs should be justified in budget explanation. Show the rationale for estimated costs.

To find out which grants might be appropriate for a particular institution, Kerr suggests calling federal agencies, contacting the school's development office, or checking with the faculty who are often on the mailing list for grant sources.

Group Advising Helps Make Do with Less

How do you advise students effectively when your student-to-staff ratio is 1:1500? That question faced advisors in the College of Business at the University of Toledo. Their solution: group advising.

"Back in 1987, three advisors saw all lower-division students on a walk-in basis," says Nancy Lapp, coordinator of undergraduate advising. "Basically, it was like herding cattle. It didn't help retention and was very unprofessional."

Mary Ormson, then the new assistant dean of student services, agreed. Coming from Iona College (NY), a school that used the group delivery system for advising business majors, Ormson took one look at UT's student/staff ratio and said, "We have to change this."

So UT implemented mandatory group advising for new day students with 48 or fewer credit hours, while maintaining individual advising for adults and those with physical or mental challenges.

They began with first-year students because "freshmen come to their first experience at UT — orientation — in a group setting," says Ormson. "We didn't want to disrupt those already in the system."

The 50-minute group sessions — servicing up to 75 students at a time — are held throughout the week at varying times, depending upon classroom availability. Students sign up for a session when they pick up their registration materials in the advising center. "If we're going to make it mandatory," says Lapp, "we have to make it available. The last thing you want to do is put up roadblocks."

During the first 25 minutes of each session, Ormson and Lapp review registration procedures and discuss specific aspects of the university. They reinforce the curriculum during the fall quarter, cover academic standards during the winter, and prepare for the sophomore year in spring. The remaining time is for questions.

"One of the things that makes the system work for us," says Lapp, "is that we've got a list of general education courses with no prerequisites." Ormson adds, "We're not advising students into particular times. We're just approving specific courses. It's the students' responsibility to figure out how the courses will fit together."

Two faculty from each of the five disciplines attend the sessions to answer questions and sign registration forms. Before each quarter, Lapp and Ormson run a training session for faculty to review transcripts and remind them about the requirements of probation.

For those concerned that group advising lacks the personal touch, Ormson points out that it doesn't eliminate one-on-one advising.

"Those who will make use of our services — the shy, those who don't want to ask questions — have a name and a face to come to," she says. Group advising also frees the staff to spend more time with those students needing additional help.

Ormson admits that group advising is more difficult with a wide variety of majors, but it can be done. "You can use a group setting for disseminating information on overall requirements. Then, when a student comes in for the appointment, you don't need to go over the general information again. You can ... do more in-depth advising."

Group advising can also be used for special populations, such as students on probation. "It's not an all-or-nothing system," says Ormson. "It's just one model that can be used in conjunction with other types."

How do the students feel about the group delivery system? The biggest complaint seems to be that it's repetitive for those who are first-year students in their fourth, fifth, and sixth terms. Otherwise, 88% rated it good or excellent on the annual questionnaire.

"We've noticed that in sophomore walk-in advising, students know how to read the checksheet of graduation requirements," says Lapp. "Before that, students didn't even know what the checksheet was." She adds: "The questions we hear are at such a higher level."

For more information, contact:

Thomas Kerr, Associate Dean of Engineering, Boston University, 110 Cummington St., Boston, MA 02215; Ph: 617/353-4447; or Nancy Lapp, Coordinator of Undergraduate Advising, or Mary Ormson, Assistant Dean of Student Services, College of Business, University of Toledo, 2801 W. Bancroft, Toledo, OH 43606-3390; Ph: 419/537-2087. (July 1992)

Alpha Gives Undecided Students a Sense of Identity

"What are you majoring in?" is the question an undecided student dreads the most. But for undecided students at

Albright College (PA), the Alpha program alleviates some of the anxiety.

Since 1983, Alpha has provided undecided first- and second-year students with guidance and an identity. Alpha got its name from the first letter of the Greek alphabet — often used to represent such concepts as "the first step" or "a new beginning."

Albright's tradition of liberal arts and the increasing career orientation of its students were the driving forces behind Alpha's development. "We wished to emphasize the value of coming to college with an open mind and settling on an area of concentration after a year or two," says John Incledon, the program's director.

Academic advising is one of the most distinctive and success-ful features of Alpha. While all Albright faculty advise students, 22 specially trained faculty members who are familiar with all of the college's majors, concentrations, and pre-professional curricula advise Alpha students. These fac-ulty represent a wide range of disciplines and are strongly committed to the program.

Once a student chooses a major, he or she is assigned a departmental advisor, unless the Alpha advisor is in that major. In addition to helping choose a major, Alpha advisors also assist in course selection.

Incledon explains why there's a need for Alpha. "We found that many incoming freshmen have a tremendous amount of pressure ... to make long-range decisions in their lives, not only where to go to school, but what to major in and what career path to choose."

He adds, "We let them know there's nothing wrong with the fact that they don't know what they're going to major in. You could say it's a support group of sorts."

Alpha also arranges special events for students and advisors, including an annual bus trip to the Smithsonian Institute museums and the Capitol Mall. Incledon explains that the Smithsonian is an informal symbol for the program because it covers nearly every area of knowledge explored by Alpha students. Workshops explaining the results of the interest inventory that students took during orientation and other career and social get-togethers foster a sense of belonging.

Since nearly one-third of Albright's 300 incoming first-year students choose the program, and fully half of those who enter Albright with a major change it before graduation, Incledon notes that an undecided student at Albright gets a lot of peer support.

Besides eliminating barriers that contribute to attrition, Alpha also helps the college recruit prospective students. Incledon remarks that what he often hears from prospects is that "we're unique and this (Alpha) is something that makes us different."

For more information, contact:

John Pankratz, Dept. of History, Albright College, Reading, PA 19612-5234; Ph: 215/921-2381. (February 1992)

Necessity Is the Mother of Invention

In fall 1990, the University of New Hampshire faced severe state funding cuts that left its advising center with the need to cut staff by 30%. The cuts forced the university to face the critical question of "how to continue to offer quality advising to 2,500 undecided students with 30% fewer workers," says Marcia Rollison, the center's assistant director. The answer: supplementing the advising staff with volunteer emeritus faculty.

UNH's advising center handles only undeclared students; once students choose a major, they're turned over to faculty in that department. Before the budget cuts, the center had four full-time professionals and 12 faculty advisors — who were paid $600 per semester for two hours of work per week.

After the cuts, the advising center trimmed its paid faculty advising staff to six. Rollison and her staff reviewed a list of emeritus faculty generated by the vice president for academic affairs, Walter Eggers, and targeted those in areas "where we were going to have cuts anyway." Before offering the positions, she got the OK from their departments.

After choosing a core group of four, Rollison put together a training session to review policy and procedures and provided each volunteer with an advising manual. Then she scheduled the emeriti for regular weekly advising appointments at the center.

Emeriti who couldn't commit to weekly sessions were scheduled during peak periods, such as preregistration. They were also offered the option of designing workshops. One retired Pulitzer prize-winning journalist, who wanted to contribute but couldn't commit the time, created two workshops: "A Writer Talks About Writing" and "What I Wish I Had Known When I Went to College." His workshops garnered such a positive response that Rollison talked him into presenting one at orientation.

For UNH, the addition of emeritus faculty has been a win-win situation all the way around. "Departments other than the liberal arts view this as a way of reaching a large body of undecided students," Rollison explains. "It helps them recruit students to their departments.

"The emeritus faculty bring knowledge and maturity to advising sessions that you don't always get with new faculty or professional advisors. And because they're volunteers, you get faculty who enjoy advising rather than those who are doing it for merit reasons," she adds. "The staff benefits by being able to go to the emeriti when they have discipline-specific questions." Another advantage: "The emeritus faculty allow us the flexibility to pick and choose, to target areas that we can't always provide expertise in."

For students it's a definite plus. Rollison explains that several of these emeriti are generalists. "They feel comfortable talking to the fully undecided students who have no idea what they want to major in or how to go about selecting one. They're willing to take the time."

Rollison doesn't view the emeriti program as a stopgap. Even if the purse strings loosen up to allow hiring more paid advisors, "I definitely think it's something we would want to continue," she says.

For more information, contact:

Marcia Rollison, Assistant Director, University Advising Center, Hood House, University of New Hampshire, Durham, NH 03824; Ph: 603/862-2064. (March 1992)

Developmental Advising "Hallmark of Retention"

In 1986, Nashville State Technical Institute initiated a developmental academic advising program and placed it in a newly created Student Development Center (SDC). Four years later, this comprehensive advising center received an Outstanding Institutional Advising Program Award from ACT and the National Academic Advising Association (NACADA). (ACT and NACADA established the award program in 1983 to honor significant contributions to improving academic advising and to share information about outstanding programs.)

Center Provides Warm Welcome to First-Year Students

Officials created SDC during a reorganization of the school's student affairs program because "we felt that the hallmark of retention was a strong advising program," says Richard Weeks, assistant dean for student development. "And we wanted a place where degree-seeking freshmen could come for the best advising that was available."

SDC is a partnership between student affairs and academic affairs. It's operated by the student affairs office, but 40% of SDC advisor salaries come out of the academic affairs budget. "In a lot of schools the attitude that comes through is 'This is my turf,'" says Weeks. "Here, our bottom line is 'How can we make our students successful?'"

The school front-loads its advising services. Every new student meets with an advisor. During the 30-minute meeting, the advisor discusses the student's career plans, reviews test scores for developmental coursework, and eases matriculation by "keying in" the student's schedule — if he or she has the right credentials — so the student doesn't have to stand in line to register.

The ability to immediately "key in" a schedule helps streamline the process. "It's not done in a hurried fashion and enables us to look at a long-range plan for each student," adds Weeks. "Plus, you don't have the problem of making out trial schedules and then having the students disappointed on registration day."

An extended advising process enables Nashville to provide a lot of student assistance with a relatively small staff. Weeks explains: "For the fall term, we can begin advising in April and have students' schedules available during the appointment. When you're not able to have a huge staff, the extended advising process is a real plus."

Advisors are generalists in that all counsel students. But each one also has a specific area of responsibility.

One advisor is responsible for the Academic Assistance program, which offers supplemental instruction for high-risk courses. The advisor consults with department chairs about learning strategies and provides a bridge between instructional and student services.

Another advisor coordinates student life activities, while a third runs the Single Parent/Displaced Homemaker program, which serves over 100 students. Still another arranges assessments with SDC's Career Life and Planning Center. The career center offers free life-planning activities to students and the community.

That's not all. SDC holds four, three-hour orientation sessions prior to each semester. They feature awareness exercises, registration procedures, and a game called "Survival of the Wisest" as a vehicle for campus tours. Though the sessions aren't mandatory, Weeks strongly encourages student participation. "Of those who attend orientation," he says, "over 90% complete the first term successfully with a 2.0 or higher GPA, which is remarkable considering 75% of those need some developmental coursework."

But what happens after the first year? After all, SDC was developed to ease the transition into college.

"After the first year," Weeks replies, "students are assigned a faculty advisor. Advisors have copies of a handbook — contained in a loose-leaf notebook that's updated each January." (Nashville's handbook won an ACT/NACADA award in the publications category in 1990.)

"Some who are supposed to go to faculty advisors do show up here," he adds. "We service them because we feel students don't need to be given the runaround. It's really the highest compliment when a student asks us if we would remain their advisor."

Because of the percentage of students enrolled in developmental coursework and the fact that many of the school's 6,000 students attend part-time, Weeks admits it's difficult to measure the center's effect on retention. "But," he adds, "we know we're graduating students. They're completing their programs and continuing their education."

For more information, contact:

Richard Weeks, Assistant Dean for Student Development, Nashville State Technical Institute, 120 White Bridge Rd., Nashville, TN 37209; Ph: 615/353-3268. (January 1991)

Mini-Advising Center Supports Undecided Majors

Does your institution attract a lot of undecided majors? Do your faculty view advising these students as a burden? Are you concerned about the quality of advising given to your undecided students? East Carolina University addressed these concerns by developing a mini-advising center staffed by retired faculty and graduate assistants.

"The center originated out of concerns for both our undecided students and our faculty advisors," says Dorothy Muller, Assistant Dean for Student Development. "Our faculty advisors — who are happy advising students in specific majors — felt uncomfortable when dealing with undecideds. In an attempt to spare faculty some of that frustration and to keep the quality of advising high, we looked for alternative ways of helping those students identify a major."

Studies show that undecided students frequently experience a lack of "institutional ownership" due to uncertain career goals. "And we know from historical data that undecideds are more likely to get into academic difficulty or not remain in school, as opposed to students with goals," adds Muller.

Nearly 75% of the students who come to East Carolina go through the General College. Muller, Assistant Dean Jo Ann Jones, and their staff take responsibility for advising approximately 7600 students — undecideds and intended majors who can't go directly into their chosen fields. Both groups are assigned to the General College for advising while completing their core curriculum and prerequisite classes.

Of the 2400 or so students who enter each year, approximately 830 are uncertain about their career goals. Before the creation of the mini-advising center, these students would have been advised by faculty from various disciplines. "If a student declares a specific major, we match the student with an advisor in the area of interest," says Muller. "Although the procedure worked well for students who had an intended major, it didn't meet the needs of the undecided students."

A faculty member contemplating retirement suggested the idea of staffing the center with retired faculty. "Because of their knowledge and expertise, retired faculty are a great asset," notes Muller. They help staff the center during registration and add/drop periods — about 20 days per term. Because students generally don't visit an advisor unless there's a need, the faculty are there during the crunch times.

Despite faculty assistance during peak times, the center still needed to be covered on a day-to-day basis. Because accreditation regulations require graduate assistants to complete 18 hours of graduate work before they could become teaching assistants, East Carolina decided to hire graduate assistants to staff the center. "We try to select those who completed their undergraduate work at East Carolina, because of their knowledge of the university. Although we haven't been (entirely) successful in that regard, all of the graduate assistants we have selected have done well," says Jones. "We have found particularly helpful students from our counselor education program who have gained valuable experience working in the center."

The retired faculty, who sign a contract committing them to approximately 20 hours each semester, receive a nominal fee of $10 an hour for their services. The six graduate students receive assistantships.

The center is open from 8:30 a.m. to 5:00 p.m. The graduate assistants stagger their shifts so that two advisors are on duty most of the time. Advisors keep records and log every visit, with a summary of any discussions. If the first advisor isn't on duty when the student returns, the student doesn't need to start from the beginning. "In order for this system to be effective, the quality of the record keeping must be high," says Muller. "Fortunately, we find that the mini-center advisors tend to keep better records than some of our regular advisors."

East Carolina's attitude of "a small college atmosphere within a large university" is highlighted at the center. "We schedule appointments at the center for students whose GPAs fall below 2.0," says Muller. "The advisors assist these students in academics. And we don't ignore those who have experienced success. Those who have earned GPAs of 3.0 or better receive a congratulatory card from the center."

Muller and Jones have received strong administration support. The center, which was established as a pilot project in Fall 1989 in response to university concern about undecided students, has become a permanently funded part of the office of Undergraduate Studies.

Each year the 700 students in the center evaluate the assistance which they receive; these evaluations have been very positive. In addition, the Office of Undergraduate Studies compares the academic performance of the undecided students assigned to the center with those undecided students who, because of size limitations, have had to be assigned elsewhere and with all General College students. The students assigned to the center have consistently performed higher (although not significantly higher) than either of the other two groups.

As resources become available, we are expanding our services. One goal is to have all undecided students assigned to the center for advisement; a second goal is to increase career counseling and major selection efforts. The establishment of the Undergraduate Studies Academic Support Center, an extension of the mini-advising center, allows students to receive various kinds of services from probation counseling to time management, study skills, or GRE preparation support.

For more contact:

Dorothy Muller, Dean of Undergraduate Studies, or Jo Ann Jones, Assistant Dean for the General College, Brewster A-113, East Carolina University, Greenville, NC 27858; Ph: 919/328-6001. (March 1990)

Theories of Relativity: Enlisting Family Members as Co-Advisors

Family members — aunts, uncles, cousins, parents, grandparents — play an important part in college retention. And separate family sessions at orientation are an effective way to reach these key people.

"All are important in a student's life," says Patricia Volp, assistant vice president for student development at Southeast Missouri State University "Otherwise the student wouldn't be there."

For the past seven summers, Volp, and the past three summers, Judy St. John, Director of the University Center for Health and Counseling, have led a series of hour-and-a-half sessions for the families of some 1500-1600 first-year students. The program helps families cope with changing roles and includes them in the retention process. While the program is billed as optional, it's the only choice for families. "The students are elsewhere registering and we don't let the parents join them," says Volp. "If they want to be involved, this is their only option."

She explains, "The reason we keep them separate is we want them to understand their euphoria or loss. For some of them, it's the first time their emotions about their child beginning college and leaving home have shown."

Although most families are extremely proud of their new college student, Volp notes, some act as co-dependents in student attrition. Family behavior often subtly encourages homesickness: for example, parents stand by the front door weeping and telling their son or daughter how much they'll miss him or her.

During the program, Volp encourages family members to observe their student's behavior for any changes that could signal potential problems. "We can't possibly learn all of the nuances of everyone's behavior, so we expect family members to know if a student is having difficulty adjusting to college." She also cautions parents to be aware of their child's psychological needs — the need for independence but also the need to know "you're always there."

Struggles for independence aren't limited to resident students. Volp notes that commuters experience the same conflicts and identity crises even though the "rite of passage" isn't as obvious.

Good Communication and Subtle Messages

Healthy relationships are based on communication, and Volp gives examples of how miscommunication can cause problems. One is particularly poignant. Volp tells her audience about the time she went away to college and her mother sold her bed. "First, I usually get applause," she says. "Then, comes the realization that that's really appalling behavior. But the message I heard was, 'Have a great life.'"

Volp goes on to explain that she grew up in a large family and her mother had just rearranged the furniture to make more room. "There wasn't a hidden agenda in the message of selling my bed," she notes.

When Volp announces that there will be a "test," she gives the audience an example of the hidden meaning of words. "Most of the time you can literally see the anxiety rise," she says. Though the instrument is a survey rather than a test, the impact is clear.

To help families retain what they're learning, Southeast Missouri State provides a resource guide that family members can pull out after midterms when the student calls and says, "Oh, Mom, there's no one here to help me." It enables family members to ask if the student has checked out the listed options. "We tell them we want to hire them to be on the school's team," adds Volp.

As part of the program, a panel of current students "tells great stories about their lives as students here," says Volp. During the last five minutes, she brings up the "real mundane things like, has the student been taught to balance a checkbook, do laundry, handle bills?"

Evaluations rate the program high. Volp admits it creates business for her office "and it's been really good for parental relationships."

For more information, contact:

Patricia Volp, Assistant Vice President for Student Development, 1 University Plaza, Southeast Missouri State University, Cape Girardeau, MO 63701; Ph: 314/651-2264. Order the survey and resource guide for $2. (January 1992)

Program Builds Academic Success for Student Athletes

Besides plying their talent on the playing fields, higher education also expects student athletes to be honor students, role models, and leaders. But too often, athletic demands overshadow academics, putting the student at-risk for failure.

The Total Person program at the Community College of Rhode Island (CCRI) provides a network of support services and an environment conducive to all-around success. Based on a similar program developed by the National Association of Directors of Athletics, the program, which began in 1989, also aids retention, says Joseph DiMaria, dean of admissions and records.

The following components form the Total Person program:

- **Early registration**, although potentially controversial, allows student athletes first choice at courses, which ensures a schedule that accommodates practice, says Donald Tencher, associate director of athletics.

- An **on-going degree audit** monitors outstanding degree requirements and assists in certifying student athletes for agencies such as the NCAA.

- The **academic counseling** component ensures that students select courses based upon requirements, not whims, and monitors student progress.

- Every two weeks, faculty are asked to fill out a **progress report** that checks on students' class attendance, assignment completion, and test scores. "It's the student's responsibility to return the form or else risk expulsion from the team or a game," says Tencher.

- A student athlete's strengths, interests, and probable job placement are identified in the **career counseling** component.

- Where necessary, faculty volunteers are recruited to **tutor** athletes who are experiencing academic difficulty. Because student athletes have lots of distractions and demands, they often need structured environments to learn how to manage their time and other study habits. Faculty are recruited to supervise the athletic **study halls**.

- As part of the program's holistic emphasis, students receive **sports medicine** information in areas such as injury prevention and rehabilitation, insurance requirements and benefits, and substance abuse and other health issues.

- The **personal awareness** component covers personal counseling and multicultural issues.

- **Faculty support** is crucial in the Total Person program. Tencher explains, "We first recruited faculty who liked a particular sport." Then, Tencher and his associates educated faculty about the multiple demands that athletes face. A special orientation and benefits, such as travel to one away game per year and new warmups, help make faculty feel a part of the team. Involving them in the program helped the program gain credibility.

How the Program Works

Once student athletes apply for admission, they receive an admissions packet that includes information on the particular sport(s) they're interested in. Data from the applications is given to the athletic department, which builds a database on potential athletes. Coaches invite them to orientation and tryouts.

At orientation, students are introduced to the coaches' expectations and the requirements for participation in intercollegiate athletics.

For those unable to attend the mandatory orientation, CCRI is developing a special video. Students will have to see the video and sign off on it or risk not playing.

The coordinator of academic advising and scheduling, a faculty member who receives six credits of release time for the position, helps athletes select courses that meet their major requirements at times that allow for the practice of their sport.

Because of the advising/scheduling system, student athletes find that their classes contain their peers. "The social link that comes with team play is only enhanced when they take classes together," says DiMaria. He also notes that if there are six students in a class who need to make up a lab, faculty are more agreeable to making arrangements.

DiMaria's office gives a copy of the course schedule to the coordinator, who then develops a roster for faculty of all the athletes in their classes. Every two weeks, the coordinator collects information on the athletes' academic progress and distributes it to the coaches, who discuss the findings with the individual athletes.

Since the program began, CCRI has seen its retention/transfer rate of student athletes increase to 74%. The college also has seen an increased understanding and commitment collegewide to retention and a better understanding of student athletes' needs.

DiMaria notes that the program has given the college a great deal of credibility among high school athletic directors and coaches — which translates into more effective recruitment. And the emphasis on academics means many athletes receive academic scholarships after they transfer from CCRI.

For more information, contact:

Joseph DiMaria, Dean of Admissions and Records, or Donald Tencher, Associate Director of Athletics, Community College of Rhode Island, 1762 Louisquisset Pike, Lincoln, RI 02865-4585; Ph: 401/333-7313. (June 1994)

What to Do When There Are Too Many Students, Too Few Counselors

The situation was critical: the state legislature had mandated a matriculation program requiring formal counselor contact and follow-up with every student on campus. The student/counselor ratio was 900:1, with some counselors having additional duties. In addition, because of a union contract, no additional full-time staff could be hired unless enrollment increased. How to comply with the mandate, work with union rules, and prevent staff burnout?

"I was desperate. I realized that we wouldn't be able to serve all of our students, especially the evening ones," says Rosemary Montijo, then Dean of Counseling, now Vice President of Student Services, at American River College (CA). To address the problem, she decided to hire high school counselors on a part-time basis.

"With the union contract, I knew our only option was some form of temporary part-time personnel," says Montijo. "The recent graduates or counselors in the community would not have the experience in a school setting, and training them could take months. High school counselors come with a body of knowledge already. They have the people skills ... and they don't leave to take other full-time jobs like our previous part-timers did."

Montijo recruited the counselors from two of the college's feeder school districts. She presented the program to the head counselors at each of the schools, as well as making presentations at district counselor meetings. Within weeks, 12 counselors were hired, trained, and on the job.

The training consists of two evenings per week with pay. During the six weeks of training, the counselors attend lectures dealing with paperwork and procedures and they also have to "shadow" a counselor-mentor until the mentor feels comfortable in letting the part-timer counsel students.

Asked how the full-time counselors feel about their high school counterparts, Montijo replies, "They're very supportive." In fact, she added, "morale improved among the full-time counselors because they can now spend more time with the students. We've been able to reduce the number of hours they need to work during the summer, and we reinstated evening class visits explaining our services. Originally, we had to discontinue those visits because we couldn't handle the students who then came into the counseling center."

After completing their training, the high school counselors work one or two evenings per week as well as during the summer. They do everything a full-time counselor does except teach counseling and guidance classes. "I treat them as professional members of the staff," adds Montijo. "They get minutes from all of our meetings, have their own mailboxes, and have access to any resources they may need."

The program is popular among the high school counselors. "For years we've told them that our students transfer successfully to four-year colleges," she remarks. "Now they see for themselves what occurs in the transition process and the importance of having articulation agreements with our receiving four-year institutions. Consequently, they are more likely to encourage students with higher GPAs to look at the community college as a viable option as they continue their education."

High school students also gain from their counselors' participation in this program. Montijo notes that the counselors take back to their respective schools information about American River College. One counselor decided to participate because she wanted to watch the progress of some of her students at the college level, so she could better counsel those still in high school.

The cost of part-time counselor augmentation was funded through revenue from the state associated with the matriculation mandate (AB3). At present, the program has been expanded to include counselors from all of their feeder high school districts.

Montijo expects that the program will improve both recruitment and retention rates for American River College. "Both groups of counselors now have a better understanding of each other's needs," says Montijo. "This can only enhance the services we provide to the students."

For more information, contact:

Rosemary Montijo, Vice President of Student Services, American River College, 4700 College Oak Dr., Sacramento, CA 95841; Ph: 916/484-8375. (January 1990)

Neglected Minorities

This article focuses on two interesting programs for students with disabilities.

Summer Makes the Transition Easy

Over 160,000 students with documented learning disabilities are currently enrolled in postsecondary institutions, according to Department of Education figures. Despite the ever-growing numbers, many LD students feel unprepared for the college experience. The Summer Transition Program (STP) at Boston University assists future students in developing a structure that helps them make a successful transition to college.

STP is a six-week program designed to provide "otherwise qualified" high school graduates who have documented learning disabilities with a thorough understanding of their strengths, weaknesses, and interests. Although created primarily for students who are planning to attend Boston University, STP also accepts students who will enroll at other competitive institutions. Thirteen students enrolled in the first summer program.

The academic portion of the program comprises a four-credit content course combined with a learning strategies seminar and survival skills workshops. Participants select a course from one of the regular summer offerings. The two most popular: general psychology and social science. "These aren't special courses," explains Loring Brinckerhoff, director of STP. "Students are completely integrated into the class." Credits earned are transferable to other schools and may be counted toward graduation at BU.

Paired with the course is a learning strategies seminar. Its curriculum: the content of each day's class. BU hires a learning specialist who attends classes and takes notes, which are then reviewed in the seminar. In addition to mastering the content, students also learn ways to improve their memorization and categorization abilities along with test-taking and study skills.

In addition to the class and the accompanying seminar, the transition program contains three intensive topical workshops. Tailored to meet the individual needs of students, the workshops cover self-advocacy, how to use the library, and word processing.

To make the transition experience as much like college as possible, the majority of students live on campus in completely integrated housing. All outings — other than a one-day field trip which begins the program — are planned by the students. A learning disabled graduate student directs after-hours activities.

Costs run $3,000 and there are some scholarships available. Initially, grants helped support STP but Brinckerhoff explains that eventually it will operate on a cost-recovery basis.

He also notes that there's an unexpected benefit beyond improving the retention of disabled students. "The program was so successful," he says, "that three students declined where they were accepted and enrolled at BU."

Teamwork

That's what improves the lives of students with disabilities at Mount Wachusett Community College (MA). It's also the reason why, in 1991, the college won an exemplary program award from J.C. Penney, the National Organization for Disabilities, and the American Association of Community and Junior Colleges.

The Team for Students with Disabilities has played an important role in contributing to the success students have experienced at Mount Wachusett Community College. Although the college has a lengthy history of serving students with disabilities, the Team is relatively new. "Because many of the disabilities tend to overlap, we found we were contacting each other a lot," says Sharyn Rice, Team member. "So in 1988 we formalized what we had already been doing on an informal basis and called ourselves a team."

Besides Rice, there are eight other full-time staff members on the Team, including the Counselor for Students with Disabilities/Section 504 Coordinator, the Learning Disabilities Specialist, the College Counselor, and the Director of Assessment and Career Services. In addition there are part-time staff who offer academic support, tutorial services, and career guidance.

The Team strives to ensure educational and architectural accessibility for all qualified students with disabilities. The number of self-identified students with disabilities enrolled at Mount Wachusett is the highest among the state's 15 community colleges. The number of students who disclose a disability has been above 20% in recent years, up from 14% in 1987.

A top priority of the Team is the development of good working relationships with the community. High school guidance counselors and special education teachers often call to refer specific students, to obtain information regarding student services, or to request a campus tour. Team members write brochures, which are sent to area high schools and to social service agencies. These brochures are also disseminated throughout the college. Presentations at area high schools and contacts with students, face to face, or over the telephone also spread the word.

During the enrollment process, after the student has been admitted, the student is given the opportunity to disclose a disability on a questionnaire. If a student discloses a disability, the advisement process is completed by a Team member. The Team member, who may be an important resource for the remainder of the time the student is at Mount Wachusett, explains the support services available and how to access them. The student is assigned to either a faculty or Team member as a permanent advisor.

After registration, the Team's next goal is to assimilate the new students into the college environment. In order to achieve the goals of self-advocacy and independence, the Team member informs the student about the availability of individual counseling and support groups, collaborates with facilities staff to ensure architectural access, and initiates informal support networks.

Team support doesn't slacken after students begin class. Students receive individual academic support services, including ongoing monitoring by an assigned faculty or Team member advisor, and the use of learning laboratories. All have access to peer tutors, taped text services, and other electronic equipment and adaptive computer equipment.

Administrative support for the group is high. The Team is involved in every aspect of the college, from writing grants to purchasing adaptive computer hardware and software. "Since many of the students require a team approach," says Rice, "it's just one of the advantages of working together. The students keep coming, so we need to make sure we service them effectively."

For more information, contact:

Nancy Kennedy, Counselor for Students with Disabilities, Mount Wachusett Community College, 444 Green St., Gardner, MA 01440-1000; Ph: 508/632-6600; Loring Brinckerhoff, Director, LD Support Services, Boston University, 19 Deerfield St., Boston, MA 02215; Ph: 617/353-6880. (October 1991)

Overlooked Minorities: Disabled Students

One of the most far-reaching pieces of legislation in recent years has been the Americans with Disabilities Act. Passed in 1990, the act "prohibits discrimination against people with disabilities in the areas of private employment, public accommodations and services, transportation, and telecommunications."

What does the ADA mean for *Recruitment and Retention* readers?

- Renewed attention will focus on facility and program accessibility, in addition to employment and promotion issues.

- Increased access to employment, public accommodations, transportation, and telecommunications will expand opportunities for students with disabilities.

- Improved accessibility to private businesses and public transportation will increase the use of campus-based educational, recreational, and cultural facilities and programs, possibly generating new income and increasing enrollments.

- Providing qualified students with disabilities with necessary accommodations will increase campus diversity.

Establishment of Landmark College
Marks Watershed in Disabled Education

Although they affect 10% of the population, learning disabilities are often misdiagnosed and misunderstood. Many people with learning disabilities are bright and capable of high academic achievement, despite labels to the contrary. Nowhere is this shown more convincingly than at Landmark College (VT), the nation's only postsecondary institution exclusively for students with dyslexia, ADD, or specific learning disabilities.

Landmark College opened 10 years ago as part of the heritage of Charles Drake, a dyslexic himself. "He's left a creative trail when presented with problems and Landmark is one of his legacies," says Carolyn Olivier, director of admissions. The school offers an associate degree plus extensive, non-credit academic courses.

The 215 students who currently attend Landmark are bright and gifted *and* have difficulty in physically processing information. They may reverse letters or numbers, forget names, or be unable to take notes or organize information.

What makes Landmark unusual is its emphasis on student independence. While other schools provide dyslexics with note-takers, oral exams, or taped books, Landmark rejects those aids. Olivier explains: "We feel, if they don't have specific skills, they may complete college, but they won't succeed in life. At Landmark, students are committed to learning how to write, take notes, read, and spell. About the only thing they may need is extra time on a test."

Although the school sports a hefty price tag — $29,000 for tuition, room, and board — students receive a "phenomenally personalized" education. The average class size is six. Faculty members provide daily one-to-one tutorials. And each student is assigned to a personal advisor whose only job is advising.

Landmark recruits most of its students through outreach and networking. Since Student Search is prohibited from releasing names of LD students, Landmark taps parents, diagnostic service professionals, and alumni. In addition, the school places ads in various magazines and newspapers in areas with a strong parent/professional referral base. Part of its recruitment strategy is educating the public about dyslexia, which it does through press releases and newsletters. A 10-minute video, shown from the student's perspective, gives prospective students a sense of the college.

Unlike most schools, Landmark hopes its retention figures remain low. "We're thrilled with the fact that our students go on to other colleges," says Olivier. "For us, high retention figures would be discouraging ... . Independence and survival outside of Landmark is why people come here."

For more information, contact:

Carolyn Olivier, Director of Admissions, Landmark College, River Rd., Putney, VT 05346; Ph: 802/387-4767. (September 1991)

Suggestions for Managing Cultural Diversity in the Classroom

Institutions serious about retention can't overlook the importance of managing cultural differences in the classroom. The backgrounds and values that faculty encounter in class — which grow more diverse each term — need to be addressed before diversity hinders learning.

Jim Hamrick, associate director of the English Program for Internationals at the University of South Carolina, offers some suggestions for faculty who want to use cultural diversity to enhance learning.

1. Each person in your classroom is a unique, special individual. The better you know your students, the more effective your instruction can be.

- Treat each student as an individual, regardless of the student's cultural, ethnic, or economic background. Learn your students' names and be sure they know your name.

- Take time, as possible, to know your students as individuals.

- Avoid labeling students. Avoid even thinking about a student as a "foreigner," a "Greek," a "redneck," or a "pre-med major" — unless the categorization helps you teach more effectively.

2. Learning is enhanced when students feel secure with the instructor, classmates, and themselves.

- Respect every student's cultural heritage and values. Require that students treat each other with the same measure of respect.

- Share your own cultural background with your students. Share cultural traits, both positive and negative. Explain how your background has affected your professional development.

- When appropriate, share your own values with sensitivity.

- Be honest about negative cultural traits — including your own — but avoid dwelling on the negatives which may be associated with a cultural or ethnic group. Every culture has positive characteristics which should be accentuated.

3. People are usually unaware of their own culturally determined traits and values until they have been directly exposed to other cultures. Only after people are exposed to other world views do they recognize their own — and perhaps become more sensitive to those of others.

- Ask questions which encourage students to examine presuppositions found in texts, class materials, or lectures. As students examine the presuppositions of others, they're more likely to examine their own routine presumptions.

- Expose your students to points of view — both academic and social — which are different from your own.

- Remind your class that academia is a specialized subculture and that successful students usually learn to function within it.

For more information, contact:

Jim Hamrick, Associate Director, English Program for Internationals, Byrnes 310, University of South Carolina, Columbia, SC 29208; Ph: 803/777-3867. (March 1991)

Center Restores Academic Hope

by Jennifer Lind

It seems all too common. A student begins college, only to find out that the intimidating red-brick buildings and 8 a.m.

classes are more of a challenge than he anticipated. Another student discovers that the personal problem she thought had ended in high school is coming back to haunt her and getting in the way of a productive college career.

Many schools have retention centers to help these students avoid academic failure. But do they recognize how a personal problem affects career goals? What about the student whose academic potential is stifled not just by poor study habits, but deeper factors?

Since 1970, the College Restoration Project at Rochester Institute of Technology (NY) has attempted to restore students to good academic standing by focusing on problems that may not immediately show through poor grades.

"Retention centers used to be more instructional, with more skill work," says Jane Munt, CRP director. "Now, we look at the person as a whole." The center's staff ask the student what he or she feels is the problem. Then they schedule the student for private sessions with a mentor for one quarter. If the student doesn't show improvement by the end of that time, Munt says, he or she is suspended from college.

The CRP focuses on three major areas: skill development, mentoring, and career advisement.

The skill development, Munt says, isn't "remedial, but developmental. We move forward from where the student is, to let them move ahead."

Students take skills and diagnostic tests when they first enter the CRP. Staff then ask them which factors have interfered with their college development.

After two weeks, students must make a decision about their own area of focus, whether it be academic, personal, or career. They are then scheduled for individualized non-credit developmental mentoring, along with a combination of credit courses for their major.

The CRP students become very close, Munt says. "The group is probably a larger factor than the mentor in making the student feel comfortable at the CRP, because students often feel alone and isolated."

The career advisement centers on a student's goals and personal factors interfering with college. Student progress is evaluated through grades, attendance, motivation, personal factors, and skills progress, Munt says. If the staff feel the student hasn't made improvements, he or she most likely will not be allowed back into school.

The CRP annually serves about 60 to 70 full-time students, some from other schools that refer students to the CRP because "there aren't many other programs like this one" that combine services, according to Munt.

The need for this approach seems to be increasing. Munt points out that the number of students needing assistance rose to 33 this quarter, which caused them to close the program due to lack of space.

The center currently serves a combination of first- and second-year students along with non-traditional students, whose increasing numbers in college require different counseling approaches.

A success rate of 60%-70% gives Munt hope that the center's innovative approach is working. "We try to give the student a certain level of self-reliance," Munt says. "So far, we've been getting good feedback. The students say the CRP helped them to develop their own autonomy, which is crucial for their success."

For more information, contact:

Jane Munt, Director, College Restoration Project, Learning Development Center, Rochester Institute of Technology, 1 Lomb Memorial Dr., Rochester, NY 14623; Ph: 716/475-2400. June 1993)

Don't Forget the Parents

by Jennifer Lind

Parents just pay their child's tuition, are too busy to get involved with the college, and aren't worth the administration's attention. Fact or fiction, Grace Severino, former director of Syracuse University's (NY) Parents Office, says parents often feel neglected in their child's education.

Established in 1972 as part of student affairs, the Parents Office functions as a central resource for SU parents who call with questions ranging from their child's academic life to campus security.

The office is unique because most colleges appear to be uncommitted to parents, according to Severino. Whether that perception is accurate doesn't matter; when parents become concerned about their child's adjustment, the Parents Office — now directed by Colleen O'Connor Bench — acts as an assurance of SU's commitment.

When office staff respond to parents' calls in a concerned, understanding manner, parents feel they're "getting their money's worth." As Bench put it in the *Parents Campus Connection* newsletter (Summer 1995), "The Parents Office is here to make our relativelly large institution more human in scale, easier to approach, and quicker to respond to your questions and concerns."

The Parents Office begins its mission early on, mailing handbooks to parents of incoming first-year students. The glossy, 28-page publication includes information on support services, calendars, and finances.

The Parents Office works "very informally," Bench says. Parents can write, call, or make an appointment to visit the office while visiting SU. Bench assures parents, "You'll discover that we're good facilitators because we're university-smart. We can put you in touch with the right office or person at once, saving you time and potential frustration."

The office supplements the handbook with newsletters and an annual Parents' Weekend, which has attracted some 4,000 parents. The parents have an opportunity to meet deans and staff members, as well as personnel from the Parents Office. Handouts, campus maps, and balloons also make parents feel like members of the SU community.

Parents have recognized the office's value and have made donations to show their appreciation. This "fund raising without solicitation" contributes to the general fund that finances the office.

Despite the office's obvious success over the last 23 years, it's almost in a class by itself. Very few campuses — George Washington University (DC), University of North Carolina, University of Missouri, and Catholic University (DC) — have similar arrangements. But Syracuse is convinced that the office is worth the expense.

As Bench tells parents in the Parents Office newsletter, "We're here to listen to you, to help you evaluate any problems you might share with us, to help you weigh your options, and to determine which campus office or service can be helpful." Then she notes, "like you, we want to assure your student a congenial environment conducive to achievement. Think of us as your partner in this enterprise."

For more information, contact:

Colleen O'Connor Bench, Director, Parents' Office, Syracuse University, 311 Steele Hall, Syracuse, NY 13244-2070; Ph: 315/443-1200. (June 1993)

Dead Lecture Society Enlivens Faculty-Student Relationships

Retention experts agree that the more students feel integrated into the institution, the greater the chance they will stay and graduate. They also agree that relationships with faculty play a substantial role in developing those ties.

Thiel College (PA) encourages faculty involvement through its "Dead Lecture Society." In 1991, John Yarabeck, the vice president for student life and dean of students, decided to organize a program that would help develop student/faculty relationships.

"The thought was to try and get faculty to meet students where they're at — in the residence halls," Yarabeck explains. "Some of our faculty had worked here as long as 22 years and had never set foot in the halls."

In the spirit of the film, *Dead Poets Society*, most of these presentations aren't on traditional academic topics. "What we didn't want is a lecture but a lively exchange of ideas in the true liberal arts sense," Yarabeck says. "For example, last year faculty presented sessions on baseball card collecting, antique cars, and ethics. Students are encouraged to ask questions, share ideas, and participate in discussions."

Yarabeck recruits faculty by sending letters asking if they'd like to participate. He adds an incentive — faculty get a free meal in the cafeteria with some of their audience before the program.

Keeping with the spirit of the film, on Halloween Yarabeck distributes to RAs and student leaders a list of those faculty who've responded and their topics. After consulting with their members, student leaders then contact individual faculty to set up a mutually convenient time to meet.

Yarabeck points out that response from both the faculty and the students has been very good. During each year, about 30 faculty are on the list and about half of them are asked to present programs. He estimates between 500-600 students attended the presentations each year.

For more information, contact:

John Yarabeck, Vice President for Student Life and Dean of Students, Thiel College, 75 College Ave., Greenville, PA 16125; Ph: 412/589-2125. (November 1992)

Finding the Answers

The Answer Center at Salt Lake Community College (UT) doesn't have *all* the answers. But it does provide basic information on admissions, financial aid, advising, and registration at times that fit student schedules and in a way that frees up advisors for more complex issues.

The Center opened in November 1992 out of the need to provide "accurate, comprehensive, basic information on student services to an ever-increasing student population," which had grown 75% in four years.

Located in a student union-like area, the Center serves both current and prospective students in a living room-like atmosphere without walls. Shannon Wadstein is the student services specialist who staffs the space, along with three hourly employees and nine peer advisors.

Training Leaves Nothing to Chance

Peer advisor training is a key feature of the Answer Center's success. After an informational interview, all prospective advisors spend two days in group exercises on team-building and communication skills.

Individuals selected from the group receive additional job-specific training — interpreting placement scores, describing registration procedures, and explaining catalogs and course schedules.

In addition, Wadstein runs weekly mandatory training sessions. "We have different questions that occur at different times during the year," she explains. "I try to focus the training on what's coming up."

Each advisor works 10 hours per week and receives an hourly rate of pay for their time. Because of the large number of applicants, SLCC limits participation to two years.

The advisors do more than answer questions. Last year they phoned new students to identify those potentially at risk. They also participated in the "Into the Streets" community service program.

Then Answer Center started out with an 8:00 a.m. to 4:30 p.m., M-F schedule, but has expanded hours of service, staying open until 8:00 p.m. Monday through Thursday. During the first two weeks of each quarter, the Center opens at 7:00 a.m. and stays open during weekend hours. Wadstein notes that "all of the student services windows are open in the evening, so students still get their questions answered."

SLCC developed the Center with funding from departmental budgets. From the reactions of students, the money was well spent. The number of students visiting the Answer Center continues to increase. During 1993, 10,987 students were assisted and contacts for 1994, were expected to exceed 15,000.

For more information, contact:

Shannon Wadstein, Academic Advising, Salt Lake Community College, P.O. Box 30808, Salt Lake City, UT 84130; Ph: 801/957-4923. (January 1994)

Retention: A Campuswide Responsibility

Ferris State Says "WE CARE"

by Terri Houston

In an effort to provide quality care and service to its students, faculty and staff at Ferris State University (MI) have banded together to form "WE CARE," a unique student assistance program.

This grassroots effort enables a variety of university employees (from the president on down) to learn about different campus departments in a three-session training program. After completing the sessions, they're awarded a WE CARE button and door sticker which allow students to identify them.

This group of faculty and staff stands ready to answer questions and/or give directions. While the group provides this service throughout the school year, its work is heavily concentrated during busy periods — registration and orientation.

The program has generated offshoots such as the WE CARE hotline, the WE CARE cart — cookies, juice, and donated items made available to the students while waiting in line — the WE CARE PROF's network, and recognition in all campus publications and directories.

Binghamton University Is "Here to Help"

by Debora Clinton Callaghan

With budget constraints on many campuses, it's often difficult to initiate programs to aid new students. In the fall of 1992, Binghamton University (NY) established the "Here to Help" program to meet this challenge.

"Here to Help" was designed as a low-cost way to assimilate existing peer advising services into a comprehensive program that would help new students adjust and increase their feelings of "connectedness" to the university.

Student and academic affairs staff developed the concept through informal conversations. A series of discussions with upperclass orientation advisors — who remembered their own experiences of being "lost" at the beginning of the semester — and feedback from new students solidified it. Binghamton's orientation office currently coordinates the program as an extension of its formal orientation.

"Here to Help" provides a way for new students to easily identify and access available services, as well as help them connect with trained students who, as "peer helpers," are involved in a variety of roles across campus. It also eliminates the stigma of asking an upperclass student for assistance.

Binghamton issues peer helpers a bright yellow "Here to Help" button and guide and includes a brochure and resource guide in residence hall "check-in" packets. An information center display and presentations at orientation help get the word out.

Speaking with One Voice

by Steve Infanti

When Roanoke College (VA) students have questions about the value of a liberal arts education or their courses, they can get the answers from anyone from the college president to the director of maintenance.

Thanks to a series of intensive summer seminars at Roanoke's new Liberal Arts Institute, faculty and staff are learning the histories of the college and the liberal arts, as well as what general education courses students need to graduate and why.

While some faculty may already know the importance of a liberal arts degree, others — staff in admissions, student life, and maintenance, as well as the Board of Trustees — may not fully understand the reasons for it.

Part of the institute is a three-week summer pilot program for 12 faculty and staff to acquaint them with the history of the liberal arts and how each course contributes to the goals of a liberal arts education. Participants will help train groups of students — "Liberal Arts Mentors," meeting with them periodically throughout the year. The summer seminars initially will be offered for three years to prepare a large number of faculty and staff.

For more information, contact:

Terri Houston, Director, Student Leadership and Activities, Ferris State University, 805 Campus Dr., Big Rapids, MI 49307; Ph: 616/592-2606; Fax: 616/592-3582; Debora Clinton Callaghan, Associate Director, Campus Activities and Orientation, Binghamton University, P.O. Box 6000, Binghamton, NY 13902-6000; Ph: 607/777-2811; Scott Hardwig, Director, Liberal Arts Institute, Roanoke College, Salem, VA 24153; Ph: 703/375-2350. (February 1994)

Mentoring Program Helps Disadvantaged Nursing Students

by Jennifer Lind

How can nursing schools encourage students to stay in school — especially if those students are also economically disadvantaged or academically low-achieving?

Three years ago, to retain such students, Georgia State University began a mentoring program that pairs disadvantaged or low-achieving nursing students with school of nursing faculty.

Judith Lupo Wold, coordinator of undergraduate programs in the school of nursing, explains the program's reasoning. "We get a lot of high-achieving students in nursing, but sometimes their heart isn't in it. This program encourages those students who have the right temperament, but who may not have the high test scores."

Wold began the current program in 1991 with Dee Baldwin, coordinator of graduate programs. The two joined forces after Wold wrote a doctoral paper outlining a mentoring model. Baldwin, also interested in mentoring, began a pilot program with Wold in 1989 for economically disadvantaged nursing students. A $250,000 grant from the Department of Health and Human Services' division of nursing helped them continue the program.

Wold attributes the pilot program's success to the relationship between the mentor and student, which encompasses both academic and personal issues. "For example, we had one student whose mother, father, and nephew all died within one year. When that type of crisis happens, students need a lot of support," says Wold.

Selecting the Students

To qualify for a mentor, students had to meet two of the following three criteria: be a first-generation student, have less than a 2.5 GPA, or come from a family of four earning less than $15,000 per year.

Students interested in majoring in nursing were invited to two meetings in their first and second quarters of school, at which they received information about the mentoring program. The 500 students who applied were invited back to a third meeting. Those who had shown the most interest by attending all three meetings and completing the application for nursing school were given top consideration.

The stringent requirements allowed Wold and Baldwin to select those students with the biggest need for encouragement. Only 15 were accepted the first year, and 12 in 1994.

Those selected attended an eight-week summer orientation introducing them to the school of nursing, clinical skills, and writing skills.

During the orientation, students received a stipend for tuition, a nursing uniform, and books, as well as the names of two faculty mentors matched to each student. The mentors and students were paired based on coping skills: a high-coping faculty member is matched to a low-coping student, for example. Students interview the potential mentors and decide who they want.

This self-determination continues throughout the program. Although freshmen and sophomores must meet with their mentor at least once per month, and once per quarter during their junior year, seniors meet with mentors as needed. Seniors also become mentors for freshmen.

While the students involved are only sophomores and freshmen, they're in leadership positions in the school. And, says Wold, they're much better adjusted than those not in the program — partly because they're more comfortable with faculty members.

"A student who feels bonded to a school early is more likely to stay," says Wold.

For more information, contact:

Judith Lupo Wold, Coordinator of Undergraduate Programs, School of Nursing, Georgia State University, P.O. Box 4019, Atlanta, GA 30303-4019; Ph: 404/651-4275. (June 1994)

Service, Satisfaction, and Advocacy: Xavier's Freshman Retention Program

Four years ago, Xavier University (OH) officials were concerned that only 82% of their freshmen were returning as sophomores. "While that was average for schools our size," says Adrian Schiess, director of freshman programs, "We didn't like it."

Hoping to improve retention, Xavier created a position where one person would act as a clearinghouse for all freshman programs. It hired Schiess, an Xavier alum and the former chair of the school's military science department as director.

The Position

Schiess soon discovered that students' problems crossed the entire spectrum of the university — from personal to social to administrative — and his position evolved into being an ombudsman for the freshman class.

Schiess found that his position yielded an unexpected benefit. "We got a bonanza of information from the students," he explains. This information led to fixing some systemic university problems. Of the 100 issues presented over the last few years, Schiess estimates that about 98 were resolved in favor of the students.

The Programs

Ninety days after being given the charge to increase retention, Schiess had in place the framework for six different activities designed around the philosophies of service, satisfaction, and advocacy for freshmen. Now, he and the university wonder how they ever did without them.

One of the first programs Schiess piloted was a faculty mentoring program. "We started with 10 faculty, who each had four to five randomly selected students," says Schiess. The mentors acted as an adult social contact, calling to talk or asking students to lunch.

Although the faculty mentoring program was successful, Schiess tested other types to see which model best met everyone's needs. Eventually, he settled on a peer mentoring program that has sophomores mentor the freshmen.

Schiess points with pride to the program's success, noting that "not at any time during the last four years did the retention rate of those in the mentoring program drop below 90%."

Schiess piloted three-credit, discipline-based, freshmen seminars using four volunteer faculty — from English, French, communications, and biology — who specifically wanted to teach freshmen. The seminars allowed faculty to do things they normally wouldn't do in their other classes — for example, dinner at a French restaurant, additional board work, lots of interaction. The seminars — eight to 14 each semester — also contributed to a 6% increase in retention — from 87% to 93% last year.

Another "bonanza of information" came from an 800 number that parents are encouraged to call if they have questions. This type of parental participation encouraged Schiess to develop a letter and a survey he sends to parents during the first semester. The survey encourages parents to ask their children a series of questions to see how well they're adjusting to school.

"When parents ask if their child knows who his/her advisor is and the student doesn't know, that's a sign that perhaps something may be wrong," says Schiess. "Doing this in the third or fourth week helps nip problems that are just beginning to surface in the bud."

Eight key administrators constitute the **freshman intervention task force**, a group that helps stave off potential problems by identifying students at-risk for dropping out. This group targets any student who has one or more of the following risk factors:

- Having a GPA of less than 2.0
- Owing the university more than $1500
- Didn't preregister for next semester
- If they live in one of the residence halls, not notifying residence hall officials that they'll be returning to the hall next semester

Usually about 80 students make it to the list each semester. The task force discusses each student's situation, attempting to identify any potential problems. The group then runs intervention, contacting particular students before registration to see if there's a problem and to make sure there's not an inhibiting factor that prevents him/her from returning.

To keep tabs on how freshmen are doing academically, Schiess distributes a class roster look-alike form that asks faculty to checkoff responses to three questions:

1. Is this student attending class?
2. Is this student participating in class?
3. Has this student achieved a "C" or better on any graded exercise?

All faculty who teach freshmen receive the **faculty feedback** form during the fourth week of school. Schiess notes that 96% of them are returned, many with more than just the names checked off. The tremendous response allows Schiess to do "triage" — calling those potentially at-risk students in the hopes of catching problems before midterms.

This allows Schiess to use the **tough love approach**, which recognizes that any given student is absolutely unique. Says Schiess, "Where one may need an arm around the shoulder, another may need a tougher approach."

Results: A Great Place

These programs caused retention to go from 82% to 89% the first year. Over the last few years, retention has leveled off at 88%. "This translates to 25-35 additional students who make it to the sophomore year in a typical class," notes Schiess. Xavier hopes to eventually expand the program to sophomores and juniors, then to eventually handoff students to career planning in the senior year.

How did Schiess achieve the cooperation needed to attain this kind of success? He explains: "Xavier's philosophy revolves around the idea of placing the student first. There's a genuine concern for the students here that causes the entire faculty and administration to think in that mind-set. Everyone is thinking how to make this place a great place to be educated."

For more information, contact:

Adrian Schiess, Director of Freshman Programs, Xavier University, 3800 Victory Parkway, Cincinnati, OH 45207-3110; Ph: 800/344-4698, ext. 3036; Fax: 513/745-2969. (December 1993)

The Rise and Fall of a Model First-Year Program

Over 16 years ago, Clarion University of Pennsylvania boasted a model first-year seminar, fashioned after the University of South Carolina's "University 101." At its peak in 1982-83, CUP's "Project Flourish" served over 300 students in 13 sections.

Despite little decline in first-year enrollment and despite research showing the seminar reduced attrition, the college taught only 68 students in four sections during 1990-1991. There were even two semesters during that 15-year period when no sections were offered. This is the story of the decline of a model first-year program.

Enthusiastic Beginnings

Project Flourish was created and implemented during 1977-78 by Charles Blochberger — the now-retired director of CUP's Counseling and Career Planning Center — and Francine McNairy — the former dean of academic support services and assistant to the academic vice president. Its purpose was to improve faculty-student and faculty-faculty relationships, as well as address Clarion's 25% attrition rate.

CUP patterned the project on University 101, which involves faculty and staff development as well as student development. Project Flourish contained a "teaching experience" workshop for faculty and administrators and an innovative three-credit course for first-year students called "General Studies 110: The Student in the University." Clarion even brought in "Freshman Year" guru John Gardner eight times over a 12-year period to lead the three- to four-day faculty workshop.

Factors Contributing to the Decline

In 1991, Clarion asked James Kole, an assistant professor in the academic support services department, to conduct research on Project Flourish, specifically to discover why participation was dropping.

Problems began, he says, when the union excluded non-bargaining unit personnel teaching the course. As a result, Kole says, McNairy had to enlist additional support from regular faculty.

At the same time, several departments experienced increasing enrollments. The chairs of those departments, Kole says, felt a strong need to keep their faculty teaching department courses.

Union and enrollment problems caused the pool of faculty eligible to teach GS 110 to shrink. And the remaining faculty were feeling a sense of burnout, partly because of the course's requirements — writing responses to the students' journal writing and serving as mentor — took more effort than other teaching methods.

In addition, administrators funded by state and federal grants expressed concern over non-reimbursement — which could have threatened their funding — for teaching GS 110. And non-grant administrative faculty wanted either release time or an overload payment, neither of which was provided.

Besides those factors, Kole says two other elements contributed to the decline. At the time, faculty were growing dissatisfied with CUP's president. And McNairy left to take another position. In 1994-95 three sections of GS 110 were being taught each semester by faculty members of Academic Support Services — where the course is housed.

That loss dealt a heavy blow to the project, Kole explains. McNairy conducted research on GS 110, in part to overcome some faculty objections that the course wasn't academic enough. More important, she shared the results with the faculty.

"She understood that, when you're starting something new," Kole says, "it's important to keep providing insight and room for people to communicate and ask questions."

She also provided continuity, Kole explains. For example, she periodically held faculty meetings to share ideas and teaching techniques. After she left, her role as course coordinator wasn't filled. "When McNairy left," Kole explains, "GS 110 was like a ship without a rudder."

Despite declining interest in Project Flourish, former and current GS 110 instructors whom Kole polled were, for the most part, positive in their assessment of it. They cited the cooperative effort of the administration and the faculty in providing a seminar that met the holistic needs of new students. They also commented on the "team-building" approach that the faculty development component offered.

Project Flourish not only brought administrators and faculty participants closer together, Kole says, it also helped faculty to learn and explore varied teaching approaches. "For many," says Kole, "it opened up a new awareness of teaching strategies."

Despite last year's low point, the future seems brighter for Project Flourish. This fall there are six sections offered, with more scheduled for spring. Kole attributes this renewal, in part, to support from Clarion's top administrators, particularly provost John Kuhn. Kole notes that Kuhn has been able to gain support for the class and has even convinced the union to let student affairs personnel teach again.

For more information, contact:

James Kole, Assistant Professor, Academic Support Services Depart., Clarion University of Pennsylvania, Clarion, PA 16214; Ph: 814/226-1872. (July 1991)

Game Simulates Freshman Year

New students at the University of Alabama at Birmingham (UAB) think that time flies — their first year lasts only an hour. To help prepare students for the distractions and diversions of their first year, UAB offers an hour-long overview of campus life called the "Freshman Year Simulation" game. Now in its seventh year, the icebreaker — which UAB offers during every Freshman orientation — enables students to meet their peers as well as glimpse the future.

The game is best explained as "an hour of mass confusion," says Kyle Puchta, assistant director of admissions. "We attempt to parallel what's really going to happen to them during their first year."

Assisted by a group of upperclass students known as the Blazer Crew, 200 eager rookies break up into groups of 20. Before the game begins, the new students fill out paperwork that helps them set priorities. "They're in charge of what they want to accomplish," Puchta explains. "For some, this is the first time. They also see it's a lot different from high school."

By setting priorities, students decide their academic, social, political, career, and personal goals, each of which is assigned points. "If the student wants an A average, that's 19 points," says Puchta. "If the student's goal is to be everyone's friend, it will take 9 points."

Why not emphasize academics? "We want them to realize that college isn't just to come here and take classes and go straight home."

Goal: Confusion

The students get only basic instructions before the game begins. The goal is to send them out in a state of confusion.

The simulation starts with a 12-minute fall quarter. Students pick up instruction sheets from tables labeled "library" or "class." They earn points by completing the required work — an opening paragraph for a speech on "Why I chose UAB" or research to find the names of geological areas. Once they turn in their sheets, there are no changes.

Distractions abound while students attempt to hit the books. Music blasts and Blazer Crew members try to lure players away from academics with activities such as homecoming and dances.

At any time during the game, Crew members can dispense cards that present students with conflicts — "missed a party and class because of mononucleosis" — and cause them to lose points. Other cards —" assisted a professor with research" or "got a date" — add points. The only rule: Crew members must help as many students as they hinder.

"Santa Claus Is Coming to Town" signals the end of fall quarter and the beginning of Christmas break. The five-minute breather lets students survey where they are and re-evaluate their goals.

Then winter quarter begins and so does basketball season. But sports aren't the only distraction. Some players may get caught when "a snowstorm hits and closes the library."

The snow melts and spring break arrives, with another chance for evaluation. Spring quarter offers students a last chance to attain their goals, despite distractions such as a limbo contest at "Springfest."

"Winning" and "losing" are measured by how close players come to meeting the goals they set for themselves. Some students find the simulation too real and become upset. "During each of the breaks, we emphasize that this is just a game and learning is the key," Puchta says. After, Blazer Crew members discuss the game with the students.

The game shows new students an accurate slice of college life and helps prepare them for the unexpected. "No matter how well you plan it, 101 things happen as you go through college," remarks Puchta. "The key is, they (students) have to decide what's important."

For more information, contact:

Kyle Puchta, Assistant Director of Admissions, University of Alabama, 260 University Center, 1400 University Blvd., Birmingham, AL 35294-1150; Ph: 205/934-8221 or 800/421-8743. (April 1991)

Academic STARS

Newly admitted African American students at Kent State University gain the academic and coping skills needed to make a successful transition to college through the "Academic STARS" — Students Achieving and Reaching for Success — summer program.

Students enrolled in Academic STARS have the opportunity — at no cost — to earn up to seven credits in liberal education requirements during the eight-week program. Participants are also introduced to resources such as the library, writing labs, and tutorial services, and learn academic coping skills including time management, note-taking, and decision-making.

Discussions on cultural differences and African American history round out the curriculum.

To make the transition easier, the university assigns each student a mentor or peer assistant who is a Kent upperclassman. The peer assistants, trained in mediation and problem-solving, live with the freshmen until the end of the summer program. During the first year, they maintain contact and help with any adjustment problems.

Out of 214 applicants, 20 were selected to participate this past summer. Participants represented various levels of high school achievement, including several who were conditionally admitted.

In addition to the opportunity to gain college credit at no cost, participants receive free room and board and a weekly allowance of $100.

For more information, contact:

Marlene Dorsey, Dean, College of Continuing Studies, Kent State University, Kent, OH 44242-0001; Ph: 216/672-3235; or Michelle Scott, STARS, Director of Cultural Diversity, Undergraduate Studies, Olson Hall, Kent State University. (September 1990)

High-Tech Future for Minorities

As of 1995, a very high percentage of the fastest-growing occupations in the U.S. have been science- or engineering-based. Minorities — particularly African Americans and Hispanics — are the fastest-growing segments of the population. Through its Integrated Partnership Program, Essex County College (NJ) combines those two facts in an attempt to bring more minorities — and women — into science and engineering.

IPP began in 1989 with a $890,000 challenge grant from the New Jersey Department of Higher Education. However, the grant program no longer exists and funding for IPP ended in June of 1992. Despite its short life, the program is a model for other institutions seeking a comprehensive way to address the shortage of minorities in high-tech fields.

IPP comprised four interrelated projects, to recruit high school students into high-tech majors, provide career opportunities in high-tech fields, and ensure state-of-the-art curriculum and equipment at Essex.

In the High School Project — the "heart" of IPP — students from five special-needs high schools (those with a high number of minority students and/or remediation courses) explored career opportunities in high-tech fields. Students were identified in 10th grade and, through a series of informal meetings with college faculty, introduced to careers in architectural technology, computer-integrated manufacturing, electronic engineering technology, engineering, and business application programming. The grant also built bridges with high school faculty and counselors by including stipends for their work with the High School Project.

Unlike similar programs, the students Essex wants weren't necessarily the best and brightest. "We weren't trying to recruit the superstars," says Mark Schuman, director of the High School Project. "We wanted kids on the cusp, where we knew we could make a difference." Most of the students came from the lower $\frac{4}{5}$ of their class.

During the first semester of their junior year, students enrolled in a hands-on, high-tech career orientation course, either after school or on Saturday mornings. As part of IPP's Technology Project, students were guaranteed state-of-the-art equipment in the course. This included robotics, computer-assisted manufacturing and networking. The classes were kept small to ensure that everyone has a chance to work on the equipment. Second semester, students focused on résumé writing and interviewing skills in role-playing and videotaped workshops and receive 10 copies of their laser-printed résumé. Two hundred fifty students took part in these workshops.

Those who showed interest in pursuing high-tech careers could take a three-credit, tuition- and fee-free course in business applications or engineering graphics at Essex their senior year. The Curriculum Project allowed students to "bank" credits in a high-tech major. Those who successfully completed the class and enrolled at Essex receive college credit.

The Cooperative Education Project, the fourth IPP component, provided internships to students between their junior and senior years. "Students were paid company minimum wage for high-tech jobs as well as half again their salary put into a special account to use for funding for college," Schuman explains. "But we had to stop this project because of the employment situation here in New Jersey. Unions were not happy when a company would lay off workers yet hire paid interns."

Despite IPP's short life, the state got its money's worth. And the Victoria Foundation seemed to agree: it's appropriated a small amount of money to continue the High School Project on a limited basis.

How successful was IPP? Although the program was designed to reach 120 students (30 each of the four years), Schuman estimates he dealt with over 300 students — "We just couldn't say no to all of those who wanted to participate." Schuman states, "the point of the program wasn't to increase enrollment at Essex," he explains. "It was to interest students — especially women and minorities — as to what was out there in the high-tech area."

For more information, contact:

Mark Schuman, Director, Humanities Division, Essex County College, 303 University Ave., Newark, NJ 07102-1796; Ph: 201/877-3382. (April 1993)

Research Yields Retention Data

How do you solve a problem if you're not sure you even have one? That situation faced administrators at the College of Du Page (IL) in 1989, when the Board of Trustees asked for some baseline data on retention.

"We never had any statistics on whether we had a problem with retention or not," says Suzanne Blasi, coordinator of admissions services and co-chair of the Committee for Student Success. So, to answer the question, COD did some research to see who comes to the college, who stays, who leaves, and why.

Blasi, Russell Watson (the other co-chair), and their colleagues surveyed over 6,000 students using ACT's Student Opinion Survey (SOS). They got back nearly 4,000 completed forms. Watson says COD had considered creating its own instrument. "But rather than redevelop the wheel," he says, "we used the SOS and added a few of our own questions. For a modest cost, it gave us a wealth of information."

In analyzing the results, Watson developed a profile of two student groups: persisters and non-persisters. Persisters are defined as those who stayed at COD and met their goals. Non-persisters attended COD for only 1 of 5 quarters.

Watson compared the communalities of each group of students and found that those who came and stayed:

- Had previous two- or four-year college experience, or had come directly from high school or the military

- Had used other college services — library, advising, cafeteria

- Had frequently consulted instructors outside of class

- Had some goals of completion

Those who came and left:

- Indicated up-front that they weren't there for the long term

- Generally weren't leaving because their needs weren't being met

- Had applied for admission less than one month before the quarter began. "This could be a warning sign that late applicants will be the first ones out the door," says Watson

- Indicated they seldom spoke to an instructor outside of class

Within the non-persister category, Watson was able to pick out those who were successful and those who weren't. "The successful ones came in, got their services, and left," he explains. "They still considered themselves COD students and when asked if they'd take a future class, they said 'yes.' " The unsuccessful ones, he says, felt unprepared for college work or had difficulty adjusting to college.

Watson found little difference between persisters and non-persisters when comparing class attendance. "Both groups attended class and experienced a high level of enjoyment," he says, "and both were satisfied with the quality of classroom instruction."

A year after the survey, COD sent the non-persisters a written questionnaire asking why they hadn't returned. The survey found that many had moved. COD officials checked the survey's validity by calling 120 students — half who had responded and half who had not.

A year after that, the college contacted 400 students who hadn't returned in two years. The college planed on doing one last "pulse-taking" this fall, for those who hadn't taken a class since 1989.

One of the surprising findings: it took many COD students more than two years to get a degree. "We need to be sensitive to the fact that we offer a two-year degree by definition but, by a practical application, it takes longer than that," Watson says.

COD plans to use the research in a staff development workshop on student persistence/success — based on the National Issues Forum model. Participants will choose a position based on the question: "Making choices for student success: how do we get the results we want?" Participants will also develop strategies for improving the experiences of COD students.

For more information, contact:

Suzanne Blasi, Coordinator of Admissions Services, or Russell Watson, Dept. of Psychology, College of Du Page, Lambert Road and 22nd St., Glen Ellyn, IL 60137; Ph: 708/858-2800. (September 1992)

Attachment vs. Independence: The High School to College Transition

Students who leave home for college with hopes of escaping the obligations, anger, and conflict they feel toward their parents may experience difficulty in adjusting to college.

Maureen Kenny, an associate professor in the department of counseling, developmental psychology, and research methods at Boston College, explains: "When students are connected to family by guilt and anxiety, they feel resentful. This type of relationship has a negative impact on adjustment to college."

In a paper presented at the American Psychological Association convention, Kenny reviewed the results of four studies she conducted that explore the way in which family relationships impede or support the transition process from high school to college.

Some young adults may perceive the challenges of leaving home and going away to school as opportunities to explore and master their environment, says Kenny, while others view them as stressful and emotionally discomforting. The differences in these outlooks can be traced back to parental attitudes.

Focusing on attachment theory, Kenny suggests that those students who feel they have positive parental support are more able to meet new experiences with less anxiety and more self-confidence.

"Having a secure base of support — knowing someone's there and available — helps you feel good about yourself," she says. "You're more able to explore the college environment with a sense of confidence."

Kenny's research is atypical in that traditional psychology has looked at leaving home from an independence perspective. "My experience used to be, and others still feel, that if a student wants to call their parents, then that student is dependent and/or immature."

Kenny notes that this attitude has been criticized recently because theories that look at people getting cut off aren't appropriate anymore. "Family is really an important support system for many people. Relationships are a source of strength — and we don't encourage cutting off the relationship for the sake of independence."

Women's Ways of Relationships

Kenny focused one of her studies on women who, because they're more relationship-oriented, are often judged as less mature and less competent. She found that women who view their parents as a source of emotional support, and describe moderate levels of family anxiety concerning separation, tend to have high levels of social competence.

Those women who describe an absence of strong, emotional support from parents, the presence of marital conflict between their parents, and moderate levels of family anxiety concerning the separation, tend to report difficulties in social competence and higher levels of psychological symptoms.

Cultural Diversity

In two of her studies, Kenny studied the relationship between parental attachment and student success in students from culturally diverse backgrounds, which are often viewed as more cohesive and interdependent. Kenny found that in the fall semester, these students "had fewer psychological symptoms if they felt that their parents were supporting their independence." In the spring semester, there was a positive relationship between academic, personal, and social adjustment among students who viewed their parents as a source of support.

Kenny contends that counselors need to be concerned with helping students identify and resolve sources of guilt, anxiety, and conflict in their parental relationships, and worry less about freeing students from the need for parental closeness or support. "Good relationships don't impede the process to becoming independent or psychologically healthy."

For more information, contact:

Maureen Kenny, Department of Counseling, Developmental Psychology, and Research Methods, Campion Hall 305D, Boston College, Chestnut Hill, MA 02167; Ph: 617/552-4030. (October 1993)

Beating the Sophomore Slump

While much of the retention literature is devoted to the practice of "frontloading," there's been little research to support the theory that similar efforts may be necessary at the sophomore level. William Flanagan, dean of students at Beloit College (WI), studied the issue of sophomore retention at 26 small, selective liberal arts colleges and found some surprising results.

Why Sophomores?

Many institutions view the first year as the *only* transition period from high school to college. Once students successfully complete their first year, many officials assume they wouldn't need the same level of support and programming as new students require.

But Flanagan argues that sophomores need as much support, if not more. "Sophomores are at the bottom of the heap for housing, classes, advising," he explains. "College is no longer new — the excitement and thrill has worn away and the reality of three more years has set in."

He continues, "If you compare the academic career to a marathon, sophomores are at the stage of hitting the wall. They've not solidified the concept of who they are. They're going through an existential crisis of 'Who am I?' "

Flanagan notes that these feelings come when students are struggling with other issues like career choice or major selection. "If they make it through the sophomore year, they're more likely to stay and graduate from the institution," he concludes.

The Research

Flanagan hypothesized that schools would experience a greater decline in retention following the sophomore year as a result of students not being totally integrated into the life of the college for academic, social, or financial reasons.

With that theory in mind, Flanagan informally polled deans at four schools similar to Beloit, whose responses convinced him of the need for the study. Flanagan then developed an instrument based on Vincent Tinto's "Student Integration Theory," which he distributed in May of 1990 to a group of 26 deans in two consortia of private liberal arts colleges and small universities: the Associated Colleges of the Midwest and the Great Lakes Colleges Association. (Tinto theorizes that students enter college with varying patterns of personal, family, and academic characteristics and skills, which are continually modified and reformulated based on interactions with the school's academic and social systems. Successful interactions lead to integration, which in turn leads to retention.)

The questionnaire's purpose was to compare the things ACM and GLCA institutions do for their students in the first and second years. "I basically used Tinto's model and added two additional variables: financial aid and environment," says Flanagan. "I also dropped one variable: institutional prestige."

He says his findings supported his hunch about a good research topic. "I found, as I had suspected, that the colleges did a long list of things for freshmen and a much shorter list for sophomores."

Flanagan received back 25 of the 26 questionnaires — for a 96% response rate. Only one school declined to participate. He credits the high response rate to professional relationships and the promise he made to his colleagues. He chuckles: "I promised them that if they filled out the questionnaire —

which was lengthy — I'd buy them all champagne after I finished the research." Flanagan made good on his promise at a recent gathering of ACM and GLCA schools.

Of the 25 questionnaires, only two were deemed unusable. He obtained additional data through follow-up calls or personal interviews with the 23 deans who completed the instruments.

After reviewing the questionnaires, Flanagan discovered his original hypothesis was true — the *average* retention rate after the sophomore year for these institutions was 75%, 12 points lower than the average following the first year.

Other major findings of Flanagan's study include:

- There's concern about retention among ACM and GLCA consortia members.

- Most of the consortia members make comprehensive efforts in the first year — "frontloading."

- His findings support Tinto's theory that student persistence is a longitudinal process.

- Ability to pay, social integration, and the influence of a significant other are important but not key factors in retention.

- Academic integration, skills and ability, and environment were found to be very significant in predicting improved sophomore retention.

- "Frontloading" is only a partial answer to the retention problem.

Applying the Research

Flanagan's research encouraged his employer to develop a specific set of activities for its sophomores. In the fall of 1991, 87 of Beloit's 260 sophomores returned to campus early for a free, voluntary, week-long program called "Crisis, Conflict, Consensus." Students worked with a faculty member — called a "convener" — in interdisciplinary groups to tackle a problem on national identity.

Little did they know when we were planning that the Soviet Union would be disintegrating as they were kicking off the program.

As part of the program, students spent a day off campus researching the problem. One of the groups, representing

Eastern Europe, traveled to Chicago to meet with representatives from the Serbian National Defense Council and the Croatian Cultural Center. Colloquia held during the week contained pertinent information to help solve the assigned problem.

Beloit officials tried to make the program as non-threatening as possible. Students could receive a letter grade, credit, or no credit for their work. But, to keep the groups responsible, each had to do a presentation at the end of the week. One group did a "Good Morning, Africa" video, while another examined the national identity question in the form of a drama. Still another developed a computer program accompanied by music.

To give some semblance of continuity, most of the conveners were also the first-year advisors. These faculty will continue to work with the same problem-solving group — in social as well as academic settings — during the sophomore year.

Flanagan notes that using the faculty as advisors makes them less threatening to students. "Advisors are expected to sit and talk about things that are going on besides academics," says Flanagan. Advisors are also responsible for helping the students come up with a Comprehensive Academic Plan (CAP).

Flanagan explains that CAP is "a dreaming process of things the student really wants to accomplish over the next five semesters." The accomplishments can be personal, extracurricular, social, academic, or overseas travel. Students have to work on their own, but advisors are expected to sign off on their advisees' CAP.

Focus on Major Improves Retention

Two more portions of Beloit's sophomore retention plan focus on choosing a major. During "Exploration Week," departments can "reach out and touch" some sophomores through open houses, symposia, and colloquia. And as a celebration of reaching the milestone of selecting a major, the college planned to institute a "Major Declaration Day," when all sophomores would declare their major.

Another effort to convey to the sophomores that they're special is a two-day retreat before the rest of the campus returns for second semester. They will be asked to think through some international issues and encouraged to look at study abroad opportunities and internships.

The college is so committed to the sophomore program that it earmarked funds out of the budget for the plan. Their belief in the program's impact is so strong that they were able to convince the college to subsidize students' room and board for the problem-solving exercise.

Flanagan believes that the sophomore year is a missing strategy for small college retention efforts. He's confident of the plan's success because it helps link the first and second years in a coordinated, comprehensive way.

For more information, contact:

William Flanagan, Dean of Students, Beloit College, Beloit, WI 53511; Ph: 608/363-2660. (November 1991)

Give Students "True" Responsibility and They'll Manage Themselves

by Peter Vogt

The philosophy behind the "Floor Standards" program at the University of Nevada-Las Vegas is simple: Take control away from residence hall students and many will try to take it back — in ways often unpleasant to administrators and students alike. But give them power to make at least some decisions, and they'll make good ones.

"The reality, at least for us, is that students are good at managing themselves when they're truly given the responsibility to do that," says Terry Piper, assistant vice president for student life.

Under UNLV's Floor Standards model, each residence hall floor sets up its own living standards, with its resident assistant facilitating the process. Students who violate the standards must answer to their peers, either one-on-one or at floor meetings.

The standards don't replace "community standards" or university rules — the school's "thou shalts and thou shalt nots," as Piper calls them. Instead, he says, floor standards allow students to make their own decisions about residence life issues like noise, vandalism, alcohol and drug use, and communication.

Giving students that kind of freedom, Piper admits, can raise eyebrows, especially among administrators, parents, housing staff, and even students. But he says that despite the difficulties accompanying the program, the "ambiance" of the UNLV residence halls has changed "from one of antagonism to one of cooperation" — and the numbers attest to the program's success.

For example, the amount of "unbillable common area damage" in the halls decreased from $50,000 in 1990-91 to $6,000 in 1992-93. False fire alarms during the same period dropped from 60 to six, and the number of judicial hearings dropped from 105 to 45.

And so far, residents who've worked under the Floor Standards model have asked to have other residents removed from floors only five times.

Nothing's Perfect

RAs have to be well-trained in the model and convinced that, with patience, it will work. Residents — many of whom believe it's the RA's job to be the floor "enforcer" when trouble arises — must also believe in the program. And they must take responsibility for making it work.

"Where the difficulty comes in is when 'critical incidents' happen," usually very early in the school year, says Piper. "When students violate the standards, or if someone does something I don't like, that's when students want to fall back on authority — the RA — to fix it.

"But we want them to understand *they* can fix it. We try to get students to see that once they're past this difficult period, things become a lot easier."

Piper says it takes time — and often a little frustration — for students to move beyond this initial period of difficulty. Success hinges on encouraging students to stand up for themselves — and the standards the floor has developed.

"Initially," Piper says, "students won't confront each other — their identities are too caught up in acceptance. It takes a while for students to recognize they're being denied something they want — like sleep or quiet — because of someone else.

"But once they reach that level, it becomes very easy for students to sit down and talk to each other, because by then they have a vested interest in how things turn out."

Experience Breeds Insight

Now that the program is established, Piper says residential life officials have a better idea of what problems to expect during the year and when to anticipate them. That makes it easier to prepare students and gives residential life staff a chance to modify the model.

"What we're trying to do is teach students that solving problems is not much harder than having honest dialogue ... if you respect each other," Piper says. "Some people have accused us of being rather idealistic. But if we can teach students that they can get their needs met without using the power system, in the long term we'll be better off."

For more information, contact:

Terry Piper, Assistant Vice President for Student Life, University of Nevada-Las Vegas, Box 451068, 4505 Maryland Parkway, Las Vegas, NV 89154-1068; Ph: 702/895-4375. (February 1994)

Residence Hall Improves Grades

by Peter Vogt

Students who live in the residence halls at Eastern Montana College have plenty of opportunities — and a few nice incentives — for getting good grades.

Residence life at EMC, enrollment 3,761, features an "Academic Support Program" designed to help students do better in the classroom. The program is comprised of four components.

Once-a-week peer tutoring nights feature paid student tutors who help residence hall students with their academic questions or problems.

Campus professionals and students present one-hour study skills sessions that teach students about managing their time, coping with test anxiety, taking better notes, and other strategies to help them improve in the classroom.

Typically, about 15% of the 500 students in the residence halls are on academic probation, according to Darren Schlepp, assistant director of Petro Hall, the larger of EMC's two residence halls. Throughout the semester, Schlepp contacts each of them to offer academic probation assistance.

Residence hall students who maintain a 3.75 or better cumulative GPA are eligible to get a single room for the price of a double — a savings of about $250 a semester. This semester, Schlepp has organized another academic reward, a spring break trip giveaway. Students earn chances in the drawing by spending time at the weekly peer tutoring nights.

The Academic Support Program was implemented in 1990; that year, Schlepp says, the cumulative GPA for the two halls rose from 2.6 after the fall semester to 2.8 in the spring. The pattern has been similar every year since, Schlepp says.

For more information, contact:

Darren Schlepp, Assistant Director, Petro Hall, Eastern Montana College, 1500 N. 30th St., Billings, MT 59101; Ph: 406/675-2333. (May 1994)

Residence Facilities and Retention

A recurring theme in retention research is that students who begin their education at a four-year college and live on campus have higher retention rates and are much more likely to obtain their degrees.

Two examples — Chatham College's (PA) Gateway program and a model program proposed at the former Mercy College of Detroit — represent ways in which residence facilities can create an effective learning environment for traditionally underrepresented students.

Gateway to a Degree

The Gateway program, designed in 1974, is for women 23 years of age or older. Women come to complete an undergraduate degree, get teacher certification, prepare for graduate programs, get a second degree, or come for personal enrichment. "This is probably one of the first programs of this type that gives special attention to the adult female student," says Annette Giovengo, acting dean of admissions and financial aid.

Fundamental to the program is the residential component. Chatham has developed specific residence halls for returning adults. Five of the units are for students who have one child under the age of 10 years. This arrangement gives the Gateway students the benefit of a seven-day, 24-hour, residential experience. The students become an integral part of the college community and take part in all aspects of campus life.

In addition to the residential portion, other components contribute to the program's success. Workshops provide career counseling and testing, an ongoing support program hooks students to mentors, and an academic resource center provides services such as peer tutoring, ESL assistance, and math anxiety seminars. The peer counselor program pairs a current Gateway student with a new Gateway student to act as a mentor.

"From my perspective," Giovengo says, "many colleges are doing the same thing, offering the same programs. What makes ours different is that all components are tailored to the audience and offered in a comprehensive way to the student population."

She adds, "Chatham's program offers the same quality of teaching, the same requirements for senior tutorial, and the same expectations as the traditional students. Gateway students get as good an education as the traditional 18-year-old." That's because "there aren't Gateway women or traditional women: there are only Chatham women."

Program Proposes Safe Haven for Learning

When schools merge, some solid programs may not get a chance. That's the case for a proposed residential learning environment for disadvantaged women at Mercy College, now the University of Detroit-Mercy.

Patterned after Chatham's Gateway program, the proposal by Jacqueline Zeff, former dean of arts and sciences, and Gilmary Bauer, assistant professor of religion and ethics, was to provide an alternative way of learning and living for the students they were trying to serve.

Zeff and Bauer proposed establishing a residential learning center to provide housing and support services to enable 40 teens and single women with small children to attend college full-time. They identified part of a residence hall that would accommodate six efficiency apartments for women and children as well as a children's play area.

Bauer explains the proposal as "a real attempt on our part to deal with the profound needs of our students. An urban residential experience is very important for adults, youngsters, and minorities. They need a new environment in which to learn."

"Mercy College is a beautiful campus in a residential area which had underutilized facilities," Zeff adds. "We were looking at how we could serve the population of students who, under our mission, we were supposed to serve — i.e., the poor, whose environment, if they lived at home, was often counter-productive to learning.

"Where you live is important in your ability to learn," she continues. "Our students needed a place to feel physically safe and where their children were safe. We started to think about the boarding school concept, which has always been for the elite/rich. We were hoping certain kinds of lifelong learning habits would be formed by living and learning together with faculty who value diversity."

Bauer notes that the program's intent was as a model rather than "to corner the market." Adds Zeff, "Our goal was to provide a quality experience and help the adults keep on towards their degree."

The proposal asked for $1.2 million funding, to underwrite scholarships and stipends, adapt the residence halls, strengthen the College Prep program, appoint a residential faculty member and an academic advisor, and develop a parenting program. Unfortunately, with the University of Detroit-Mercy merger, it "got lost in the shuffle," says Bauer.

Both Zeff and Bauer believe in the proposal's ability to improve retention and change students' lives. As Zeff points out, "education has always been about empowerment."

For more information, contact:

Diane Reed, Dean of Enrollment Management, Chatham College, Woodland Rd., Pittsburgh, PA 15232; Ph: 412/365-1294; Jacqueline Zeff, Dean of the College of Arts and Sciences, University of Michigan-Flint, Flint, MI 48502; Ph: 810/762-3234; Gilmary Bauer, Assistant Professor of Religion and Ethics, University of Detroit-Mercy, 4001 W. Nichols Rd., Detroit, MI 48221; Ph: 313/592-6137. (April 1994)

Survey Measures Transition Stress

by Jennifer Lind

It may seem like common knowledge that a student who feels emotionally supported in his or her endeavors will do better academically than a student without that support. Forsaking blind faith, however, members of the University of Washington-Seattle's psychology department decided to prove this "obvious" notion last June.

With the help of the admissions office, the team randomly sent questionnaires to 600 high school students planning to attend the university. The team received back 310 surveys, of which 280 were usable.

The team mailed additional questionnaires during the third week of the first month on campus, and plans to send another questionnaire at the end of the year.

"Other school surveys focus on when the students are in college, such as the first two weeks. We felt that we were missing the stress that occurs before college. All the factors — moving away from friends and family, facing a more challenging academic environment — combine to make that transition very stressful," says principal investigator and doctoral student Regan Gurung.

"One finding is that the more students perceived support, the more adjusted they were to college and the more likely to do well," says Gurung, who worked with two colleagues in the psychology department.

The survey team used four- and six-point scales to rate the level of perceived support. The questions came from department surveys and published surveys, including the Rosenberg self-esteem scale. Students answered questions about their support "network," such as the number of perceived "close" friends and relatives. They also answered "measurement" questions, such as how often they ask their friends for advice.

The team had a "ready-made" support structure to judge how student satisfaction relates to support. The team worked with the "Freshman Interest Group" (FIG) program, in which first-year students meet with peers to talk about course material after class. These groups, led by upperclass students, are optional.

The team noticed a significant difference between those who joined FIG groups and those who didn't. "Those who joined rated themselves as more outgoing after a month in FIG than before they joined, and perceived more support," says Gurung.

Although the preliminary results of the questionnaire prove the team's hypothesis, team members hope to investigate other factors next year, such as how fraternity and sorority membership and sports activity affect satisfaction. They also plan to measure grades versus perceived social support.

However, Gurung isn't sure if the team will receive enough funding to do so. The $1,600 cost of this year's survey was funded by the psychology department, the office of educational assessment, and the Sigma Xi science society.

Gurung is hopeful that other schools will look at how student support affects achievement and retention as the questionnaire is refined. "We want to look at how, and if, people who perceive low support will have problems down the line," says Gurung. "That's something schools should care about."

For more information, contact:

Regan Gurung, NI-25, Dept. of Psychology, University of Washington, Seattle, WA 98195; Ph: 206/543-6869. (March 1994)

Volunteers Strive to "Advise Five"

by Jennifer Lind

With continued budget constraints facing many colleges and universities, administrators are under pressure to develop innovative yet inexpensive programs. When that pressure affected student advising at the University of Maryland-College Park, officials looked within for answers.

Five years ago, administrators in the Division of Letters and Sciences began a program called "Advise Five," a decentralized approach to advising. Betty Beckley, assistant dean and director of letters and sciences, points out that the program was a way to combat budget pressures while meeting students needs.

Advise Five consists of 225 voluntary advisors from the 12 schools, who each meet with five first-year, undecided students. About half of the volunteers are faculty, while others are graduate students, undergraduates, or admissions and administrative affairs staff.

Volunteers learn about the program from articles in newsletters, mailings, and the student newspaper. After a two-day summer training session on UM policy and requirements, they're asked to meet with students at least twice per semester according to each student's needs.

With only five students each, the volunteers can advise the students while working at their regular jobs, says Beckley. "We work on finding volunteers who really want to work with students from as many different parts of the campus as possible."

Wendy Whittemore, Associate Director of the Division of Letters and Sciences, says, "It helps to have volunteers from different areas" outside Letters And Sciences because "students go in so many directions." Although first-year students are assigned advisors based on surveys of their interests in college, they can switch advisors if their decided major is out of the range of the advisor, says Whittemore. There's also a hotline staffed by seven professional advisors, to provide students with answers to tougher questions.

Students anonymously evaluate the volunteers at the end of each semester, says Whittemore. Last semester's evaluation showed that 90% felt helped, she says, and three advisors have maintained relationships with students into their second year.

Although most of the students are satisfied with the program, administrators hope to eventually have 400 to 500 volunteers, to ease the burden of managing the program, says Beckley. "We want students to feel supported. Part of the problem is there are so many different kinds of advising. We really work towards consistent communication, in order to promote the atmosphere of a smaller campus."

For more information, contact:

Betty Beckley, Assistant Dean, Division of Letters and Sciences, University of Maryland-College Park, 1117 Hornbake Library, College Park, MD 20742-4315. (March 1994)

Scholarship Requires a Commitment to Diversity

by Jennifer Lind

As many institutions strive to achieve multiculturality, "diversity" is turning into a catch-all word. But how can schools attract and reward students who want to contribute to an atmosphere of diversity?

In 1992, Hamline University (MN) found a way. Qualified candidates receive a merit-based presidential scholarship after demonstrating academic aptitude and writing an essay on diversity.

The scholarship is designed to attract students from diverse backgrounds to the urban St. Paul campus, where the student body is 14% minority. According to its instructions, the scholarship's essay derives from Hamline President Larry Osnes' fall speech. Echoing college administrators across the country, he stressed the need to "ensure social awareness and the healthiest of university communities" through ethnic, geographic, gender, age, and socioeconomic diversity.

"We are able to draw in great candidates," says Brian Peterson, senior associate director of admission. Although the applications are time-consuming reading for the selection committee, he says, the college is dedicated to attracting students from varied backgrounds. "The essay makes them think," he explains.

The scholarship application differs from previous scholarships by requiring students, in a 1000-word essay, to explain their views on diversity and how they will contribute to the diversity of Hamline University

The admission staff reviews roughly 140 applications and essays for clarity, argument, and academic content. The committee selects 60 finalists, who are then pared down to 20 scholarship recipients. Those students are awarded renewable scholarships from $3,000 to full tuition, depending on financial need. The scholarships, says Peterson, attract students "who are willing to tackle an issue that they may have never thought about before." Although they prefer students from the top 5% of their high school class, the selection committee may "split hairs if the applicant is 10 out of 70, but has a 3.9 grade point average."

The quality of a student's argument may also win over a committee. "A student may not totally agree with our views of diversity," says Peterson, "but if the student presents a good argument, we will consider him/her as a serious candidate."

The 60 finalists visit the campus for an interview. The on-campus interview allows faculty/student committees to "ask some pointed questions," says Peterson. "We want to bring in candidates who have thought about this, not just swallowed 'P.C.' thinking hook, line, and sinker."

For more information, contact:

Brian Peterson, Senior Associate Director of Admission, Hamline University, 1536 Hewitt Ave., St. Paul, MN 55104; Ph: 612/641-2207. (March 94)

An "Electronic Forum" Gives Voice to the Silent

by Clay Schoenfeld

"Most of the time, writing in college is done for evaluation," says Karen Schwalm, an English instructor at Glendale Community College (AZ). Schwalm preferred that her students "write to learn."

She sensed that if there were some way to combine an old, proven method of instruction — the journal — with the ease and anonymity of electronic technology, then students, especially those with weaker interaction skills, might more readily communicate with each other, particularly if they could use assigned pseudonyms.

She approached the then director of GCC's High Tech Center, Christopher Zagar, to see if the journal concept could be adapted to an electronic environment. Zagar assured her the capabilities were there, and so the "Electronic Forum" was born.

Using GCC's DEC VAX machine, Zagar set the project up to integrate student records with Forum entries. His program also included the ability to record the number of entries, words per entry, and subject area, all linked to a student's ID number, as well as a way to allow students to change their pseudonyms if they wished.

Schwalm suggested that each student make at least 15 entries during the semester, with a minimum of 100 words per entry. The electronic nature of the Forum allowed it to operate seven days a week, 24 hours a day. Students could participate at their convenience.

Traditional journals tend to be one-on-one interactions between student and instructor. Since electronic entries are read by all students in the class, students can compare the caliber of their writing with that of their peers anonymously, which lowers student apprehension. Students feel free to analyze, praise, or criticize entries, as well as to make themselves available for such reactions in turn.

The Forum extends class discussions and functions much like a student union at a residential four-year institution, a gathering place for an exchange of ideas in a less formal setting, says Schwalm.

Students — even the formerly silent ones — become "addicted" to communication, she reports. While each student is required to write 1,500 words a semester, students generally average 3,500 words.

If the adoption of an innovation by others is a sign of success, then the Electronic Forum is a winner. What began in 1989 with one instructor and 35 students on one campus now encompasses 300 instructors and an average of 8,000 students per semester on all 10 Maricopa County Community College District campuses.

"One of the biggest draws is that students can communicate with friends at other schools who have email addresses," Schwalm says. By doing so, "students set themselves on a trajectory that they may not have considered before, rather than just keep relationships with their neighborhood friends who haven't gone on to school."

For more information, contact:

Karen Schwalm, Glendale Community College, 6000 W. Olive Ave., Glendale, AZ 85302; Ph: 602/435-3651. Email: Schwalm@gc.maricopa.edu. (November 1993)

Editor's note: an article by Timothy Sloan in the Educators' Tech Exchange *contributed to this story.*

Computerized System Improves Advising, Saves Money

Computerizing a manual system can improve efficiency by reducing time-consuming personal contacts. But often those contacts play a major role in student retention. Robert Morris College (PA) has computerized part of its student advising process without losing critical, personal contacts.

The college developed an in-house, computerized student records management information system that combines processing of admissions, registration, and automated transcripts, as well as student advising and academic auditing. For its ingenuity, Robert Morris received the $10,000 top award in the National Association of College and University Business Officers and USX Foundation's annual Cost Reduction Incentive Awards Program.

The heart of the system is the automated academic checksheet listing the required courses each student needs to complete for a particular major. Each major has its own academic checksheet. The checksheet used at the time a student declares a major remains in effect until the student changes majors or graduates.

The system matches each student with his or her checksheet and tracks progress from enrollment to graduation. "The system decreases the amount of paperwork and increases office efficiency," says Frank Perry, executive director of the academic services center, and "increases the quality of the time advisors spend with students."

If a student considers changing majors, the system can — in seconds — move all prior courses from one checksheet to another, immediately identify which courses will meet the new degree requirements, and list separately those that don't.

The system also aids prospective students interested in transferring to Robert Morris. All transfer credits are input directly into the computer, and an admissions counselor can immediately tell students how many of their courses apply to any or all of the majors the college offers.

The system runs on a mainframe computer, accessible to about 130 faculty advisors and professional staff. Since the college already had an administrative computing system in place with terminals in appropriate offices, there was little cost in implementing the checksheet.

In addition to improving advising quality, the new system also improves accuracy. Three years ago, a variance in recordkeeping led the registrar to install an expensive micrographics system to produce transcripts. With the automated checksheet, Robert Morris has eliminated the micrographics system for transcript production and reduced personnel time.

And, of course, the checksheet saves money. Officials estimate that the system saves over $78,000 annually through decreased dependency on faculty advisors and reduced clerical time.

For more information, contact:

Frank Perry, Executive Director, Academic Services Center, Robert Morris College, Narrows Run Rd., Coraopolis, PA 15108-1189; Ph: 412/262-8422. (March 1991)

College Makes Students "Job 1"

You've heard the slogans — Ford's "Quality Is Job 1" and Andersen Windows' "Come Home to Quality." Beset by global competition and lagging sales, growing numbers of businesses have adopted W. Edwards Deming's 14 principles of Total Quality Management. With the exception of a few schools — including St. John Fisher College (NY) — colleges and universities have, so far, resisted the change.

But there are signs that higher education is listening. In an article in *Business Week*, Gary McWilliams notes, "After decades of jealously guarding their turf, colleges and universities are on the verge of transformation. Pressured by dwindling enrollments and budget woes, a small but growing number of schools are looking to business and adopting techniques, strategies — even the language of quality management."

Assumption: Workers Want to Do a Good Job

Deming, an American, created "Total Quality Management," which the Japanese successfully used to rebuild their industries after World War II. Though best known in manufacturing, his principles have also worked well in the service sector. TQM's key elements include continuing improvement, assuming workers want to do a good job, and staying close to customers. TQM empowers workers, holding that those closest to customers and processes know them best.

Peter Lindsey, dean of admissions, explains how St. John Fisher, a small liberal arts college, found itself in the forefront of change. "There are very few colleges nationwide involved in TQM," he admits. "But in Rochester, we have Eastman Kodak and Xerox, both ... heavily involved in the process. In fact, Xerox recently received the Malcolm Baldrige award for quality."

He continues, "We make a promise to prospective students that says, 'If you come here, you'll be treated with exceptional personal attention and service.' For a college of our size and type, TQM sounded like something we should be doing."

So several years ago, the college invited a Kodak executive to instruct directors and senior staff on TQM's intricacies. Lindsey describes the executive as receptive, knowledgeable, and curious about how TQM could be applied to higher education. "The executive didn't have a blueprint any more than we did about implementing the principles in higher education," he says. "But we forged a good marriage." From those meetings, a variety of departments — including the admissions office — began to implement Deming's principles.

Implementing TQM

The admissions office first identified its internal and external customers. Lindsey notes there was some initial resistance to identifying students as "customers." "But," he adds, "whether we call them 'students' or 'customers,' we need to treat them well and make sure we are serving their needs as effectively as we can."

This "customer service" perspective led the admissions staff to step two — developing a mission statement. "Our mission statement has an objective, a means of accomplishing the objective, and an outcome."

Identifying critical processes is the third step in TQM. "One thing that Deming stresses," says Lindsey, "is that success isn't a matter of doing many things. It's a matter of doing what's central to your job. The key is to focus a majority of your time on the things that will have the greatest impact on meeting the needs of your internal and external customers.

"When you analyze problems carefully, what you discover is that they're much more complex than they seem at first," he explains. "Usually people try to tackle complex problems with a one-hour meeting, which results in Band-Aid solutions. But they haven't really understood the problem, the process, or how to fix the process."

For example, Lindsey notes, the registration team worked on its report for almost two years, using the TQM problem-solving approach to identify its customers, processes, and problems. "You think that registration is fairly complex," Lindsey says. "But you don't understand how complex until you flow-chart it. I'm amazed there aren't more mistakes or poorly served students because of its complexity."

One of admissions' early TQM projects was to improve mail turnaround time. A cross-functional Q (for quality) team, made up of representatives from college communications, data entry, admissions, and the mail room, studied the processes and made some changes. Since then, the college has dramatically reduced the time it takes to get some 20 publications to each of its 18,000 inquiries.

The college assembled another Q team to study the problem of restricted scholarship aid, to ensure that it was offering and expending 100% of the money. "Our donors need to see scholarships awarded to students who meet their criteria," says Lindsey. The result: happier donors and significantly better distribution of scholarship funds.

Lindsey admits that, in the short run, TQM is an investment of time. "When you address problems, you find they're more complex. Problem-solving is slower, which can be frustrating. But in the long run, you find better solutions and you end up serving people better."

For more information, contact:

Peter Lindsey, Dean of Admissions, St. John Fisher College, 3690 East Ave., Rochester, NY 14618; Ph: 716/385-8064. (January 1992)

Also see:

"A New Lesson Plan for College," *Business Week*, Oct. 25, 1991.